Sudo-Q

This book is published to accompany the series
Sudo-Q produced for BBC Daytime by
BBC Manchester Entertainment
Executive Producer: Sumi Connock
Executive Editor: Martin Scott
Production team: Pam Cavannagh, Gareth Edwards, Michelle Lanaway, Denise Harrington-Harrop, Lyndon Saunders, Dylan Pierce, Jon Kelly, Ben Armstrong, Rachel Harrison, Sue Fletcher, Julie Corcoran, Charlotte Faux, Emma Parsons, Erin MacTague, Stephanie Page, Robin Owen Ellis

First published in 2006 by BBC Books
BBC Worldwide Limited, Woodlands, 80 Wood Lane,
London W12 0TT

ISBN-13: 978 0 563 49394 5
ISBN-10: 0 563 49394 1

Commissioning editor: Vivien Bowler
Project editor: Eleanor Maxfield
Proofreader: Vicki Vrint
Designer: Jo Ridgeway
Production controller: Arlene Alexander
Researcher, introductory text: Sally Palmer, Deputy Editor
BBC Focus Magazine (www.bbcfocusmagazine.co.uk)

With many thanks to Su Doku enthusiasts Margaret Miles, Mickey Miles, Fiona Nerberg, Lynne Maxfield and Steve Maxfield.

Set in DIN and Reaction Ultra
Printed and bound in Great Britain by Clays Ltd, St Ives plc

For more information about this and other BBC books,
please call 08700 777 001 or visit our website at www.bbcshop.co.uk

Sudo-Q

Introduction by Eamonn Holmes

Sudo-Q: Welcome

Sudo-Q is the book that takes Su Doku a step further by adding a healthy dose of general knowledge. It's an interesting and challenging way to improve your logic expertise, learn to tackle harder grids and test all areas of the brain at the same time – you can even try the grids against the clock!

Just like the BBC television programme that I present, this book can test you in several ways. In the programme, the contestants' wits are put to the test as they battle it out to complete grids over four tense rounds. If they answer a general knowledge question correctly, they earn the right to tackle a grid. Now here's a book based on the principles of the show so you can play along at home, pushing your Su Doku skills to the limit.

This is how it works. Su Doku is normally played in a 9 x 9 square grid (a 3 x 3 grid of boxes each containing a grid of 3 x 3 cells). Each cell holds a digit from 1 to 9, subject to a few rules:

Each horizontal row can only contain one of each digit.
Each vertical column can only contain one of each digit.
Each 3 x 3 box can only contain one of each digit.

That's all there is to it numerically! But where do the general knowledge questions come in?

Sudo-Q: Know how with know-how

In each of the Su Doku grids in this book, the letters A, B and C also appear. These three letters correspond to the general knowledge questions underneath the grid. If you choose the right multiple-choice answer, you will be able to fill in an extra number on the grid to help you solve the puzzle.

7			5					
	A				8	9	1	7
	3			4		6		
1				B	5	4		
		2	4		9			
	5			8			9	1
		4		7		3		9
		1		5			8	
	9	7	6				C	5

For example, question A has three multiple-choice options, but only the correct answer will provide you with the correct number to pencil in over the 'A' square. The incorrect answer will sabotage the grid, so, as with a normal Su Doku puzzle, take care if you are guessing!

The book is divided into four Japanese-themed rounds of increasing difficulty: Apprentice, Warrior, Shogun and Emperor. You can tackle the grids in your own time or against the clock. And you can play on your own or in competition with friends. Read our 'Three ways to use this book' section to discover the best approach for you!

Sudo-Q: The background

Su Doku is a number-based game that has its roots in a game called Latin Squares, developed by Swiss mathematician Leonhard Euler in 1783. Latin Squares took the form of a grid, and every number and letter in the Greek alphabet had to appear once in every line and every column.

Despite its mathematical origins, Su Doku uses logic rather than maths, so there is no need to be put off, even if you find maths difficult. The numbers 1–9 are used for convenience – you could just as easily use letters or symbols. The difficulty depends on the positioning, and amount, of the numbers you're given to start with, but a true Su Doku puzzle will only ever have one solution.

The puzzles in their current form were first published in 1979 by US company Dell Magazines, under the name 'Number Place'. They were designed anonymously by a 74-year-old retired architect called Howard Garns. In April 1984, Japanese company Nikoli adapted Dell's puzzle for a Japanese audience, and it quickly became a craze there. It only caught on here in the UK after a retired High Court judge, Wayne Gould, came across the puzzle while on holiday in Tokyo in 1997 and brought it back with him. He spent six years developing a computer program to generate the puzzles, and turned them loose.

As the Su Doku craze has deepened, more variations of the basic 9 x 9 game have evolved. You can now get grids with 4, 5, 6, 7, 9, 16 and even 25 cells along each side. Some variants add a third dimension, so your puzzle is cube-shaped rather than square and each row or column spans two faces instead of one. It's even possible to have a 'magic' Su Doku grid, where at least one 9 x 9 box in the grid is designed so that all the rows, columns and diagonals add up to the same 'magic' number.

Today, there are Su Doku clubs, online Su Doku chat rooms, and endless strategy books, as well as videos, mobile phone games, card games and competitions around the world. And now there's Sudo-Q! Whatever type of Su Doku game you enjoy, hopefully these tips and tricks will make it easier to solve them. Happy puzzling!

DID YOU KNOW?

The name 'Su Doku' was coined by Maki Kaji, president of Japanese company Nikolai who introduced the game to Japan in 1984. The puzzle's name was 'Suuji wa dokushin ni kagiru', which means 'the numbers must be single'. It was shortened to Su Doku: Su = number; Doku = single.

In July 2005, Sky One claimed they'd constructed the world's largest Su Doku puzzle, on a hillside near Chipping Sodbury. It measured 84m^2 (275 square feet), and they offered £5000 to the first person to solve it. But that puzzle was later found to have 1905 solutions, so did not officially count as a true Su Doku.

Three ways to use this book

Want to Improve?

Sometimes it can feel as if everyone around you is part of an exclusive Su Doku club. If you've been working away at simple Su Doku puzzles with your cup of tea for some time, but just can't seem to crack the more 'serious' puzzles, then this book could help you along. You can use the questions in this book to give your mind a break from mind-boggling numbers, to give you a boost when you get stuck and to help you get used to the different patterns found in more complicated grids.

YOU NEED AN 'IN'

Su Doku is just like any other logic puzzle: it takes practice, and yes, you can train yourself to get better. Not only that, but the more training you do, the cleverer you'll become. Scientists have proved that by focusing on a logic puzzle for half an hour every day, you can significantly improve your IQ. Many people give up because they just don't know where to begin. But there are three rules that should always get you started and will help you to overcome every hurdle.

The first rule of Su Doku Club: Elimination

5	4	A	2		3	1		9
		7						
	8							

Which digit can go in cell A? It can't be 1, 2, 3, 4, 5 or 9 since those digits have already been placed in the top row. It can't be 7 or 8 because those digits are already placed in the same 3 x 3 box. So it must be 6.

The second rule of Su Doku Club: Placement

	2					A	B	C
				2		D	E	F
						3	G	4

Rule 2 is about finding a home for a digit that must go somewhere. We know that the right 3 x 3 box must contain a 2, but where? The top and middle rows already contain a 2, so we can eliminate them. The only place the 2 can go is cell G.

The third rule of Su Doku Club: Constraint

5	2	7				8	3	1
A	3	4				2	9	5
B	8	9						

Sometimes, even when a digit can go in more than one cell in a box, you can still use that fact to position a digit elsewhere. We know that the right-hand box must contain a 6 somewhere in the bottom row. This means the bottom row of the puzzle contains a 6, so in the left box, the 6 must go in cell A.

HERE'S YOUR TARGET

The key to starting off with Sudo-Q is to do as much as possible, even if that means making more mistakes! This book has several levels of difficulty so you can take the small steps needed to improve.

The earlier grids in each section have easier questions. If these answers are obvious to you, take the helping hand gratefully, giving yourself a few extra numbers in the grid to start off with. Once you feel you don't need the extra help, move on to grids with more challenging questions ... or don't look at the questions at all!

Some people swear that the easiest way to do Su Doku is to write all possible numbers in every cell before you start. You then cross them out as you eliminate them from each square, finally leaving you with the correct one. However, you may find you don't need to do this on easier puzzles and it can get confusing unless you've photocopied your grid extra-large to give you enough space to write in. A better trick is to write only in the top of a cell if there are just two possible numbers that you're not sure about for that cell. That way, there aren't numbers and crossings-out all over your grid.

When you feel yourself getting better (and you start to notice a cleaner page!) take it as a sign to move on to the next round in the book.

Want a Challenge?

If you've watched the show or have cracked a few puzzles in your time, then you're probably already addicted to Su Doku. But we all need a new challenge. The Warrior and Shogun rounds of the book should really put your logic skills to the test. Those of you who regularly play at home or tackle a puzzle a day should try our challenging Emperor section at the back of the book.

To make it all the more interesting, the questions in every round get harder as the number of the grid goes up (i.e. grids Apprentice 1–10 are easier than Apprentice 11–20, and Apprentice 21–30 are harder still).

YOU NEED A FULL BRAIN WORKOUT

Part of the challenge of the television show is to swap from answering general knowledge questions, to focusing on the grid as players 'earn' their chance to fill in the cells. There are just a few seconds to scan the numbers again, refresh the patterns in your brain and start cracking the code. Swapping in between the two is a great way to learn how to 'multi-task' and work the different areas of the brain.

HERE'S YOUR TARGET

You can refer to our time-challenge table below to set yourself targets. It will help you to judge your ability and an idea of what to tackle next. Simply time yourself from beginning to completion of the grid and see how powerful you have become!

Grids	Time taken	Tip
Apprentice 1–10	under 5 mins	try Apprentice 21–30
Apprentice 11–20	under 10 mins	try Apprentice 21–30
Apprentice 21–30	under 10 mins	try Warrior 11–20
Warrior 1–10	under 10 mins	try Warrior 21–30
Warrior 11–20	under 15 mins	try Warrior 21–30
Warrior 21–30	under 15 mins	try Shogun 1–10
Shogun 1–10	under 15 mins	try Shogun 21–30
Shogun 11–20	under 20 mins	try Shogun 21–30
Shogun 21–30	under 20 mins	try Emperor!

If you can complete an Emperor grid in under 30 minutes you are officially a Sudo-Q genius. Take a quick break to tell the world before going straight back to the beginning to complete ten Apprentice grids in 30 minutes!

Want to Compete?

For those of you who cannot resist the bloodthirsty urge to compete with other Su Doku champions, this book can turn your one-man puzzle into a challenging tournament just like the television programme!

YOU NEED A 'HEAD TO HEAD' CHALLENGE

Try this simple game. Players compete in rounds against the clock. Start off on an Apprentice puzzle and set the timer for 10 minutes. At the end of the time limit, players get one point for every correct number they have entered into their grid.

For example, if player one has filled in ten new numbers, they get ten points. If any players complete the grid in the time limit, they get the maximum points including the bonus of those numbers already given in the puzzle to start off with (45). If any incorrect numbers are entered, points are deducted. It is possible for players to end up with a negative score!

Compete in this fashion through the Warrior and Shogun rounds. Allow 15 minutes for the Warrior puzzles and 20 minutes for the Shogun puzzles. At the end of the three rounds, tally the total number of points for each player.

HERE'S YOUR TARGET

There can only be one Emperor, so you need to face the Emperor stand-off final. The two players with the highest scores go head to head and tackle an Emperor grid. Remove the time limit as the two Sudo-Q geniuses compete to finish the grid correctly in the quickest time possible. If any number is incorrect they are immediately disqualified, and the other player wins the game.

If you are playing with two players only, simply tackle an Emperor puzzle in 30 minutes and add to your final score. The player with the highest score is the champion.

(NB If, at any point in the game, a tie-break between players occurs, a different player must ask them a general knowledge question from any other puzzle in the book. The first player to shout out the correct answer goes through.)

Sudo-Q: Satisfaction

I feel it's a shame to spend a lot of time and effort completing a puzzle unless you pause to congratulate yourself afterwards. Whether it's putting a smile on your face, boasting to your neighbour or treating yourself to a slice of cake, you should feel as successful as any of the contestants on the television show and reward yourself. The general knowlege questions are, essentially, a fun twist to a popular logic puzzle and should provide you with the ultimate Sudo-Q satisfaction.

I hope you enjoy the book as much as I enjoy presenting the programme!

Eamonn Holmes, 2006

Round One

7			5					
	A				8	9	1	7
	3			4		6		
1					5	4	C	
		2	4		9			
	5			8			9	1
		4	B	7		3		9
		1		5			8	
	9	7	6					5

1 apprentice

A In the field of education, what does the abbreviation PTA stand for?

Parent Teacher Association 4

People's Training Association 2

Personal Teaching Assistant 6

B Which of the Brontë sisters wrote the novel *Jane Eyre*?

Emily Brontë 1

Anne Brontë 2

Charlotte Brontë 8

C What is the nickname of Lancashire and England all-rounder Andrew Flintoff?

Chalkie 7

Toffie 3

Freddie 6

2

apprentice

	9				3		8	C
1		6	2	7		9		3
4		5			8		7	
2		7	8		9	5	6	
3		8	1		6	4	9	
	A			5				8
	6			B	7		2	
5		3	4	6		8		9
8		4			1		5	

A What nickname was given to the Boeing 747, which, when it came into service in 1970, was the world's largest passenger airliner?

Flying Fortress 2

Jumbo Jet 1

Spruce Goose 4

B Atlanta is the capital of which US state?

Georgia 8

Florida 3

Texas 9

C In football, what term is used when a player passes the ball through an opponent's legs and then nips round to collect it again?

Parsleying 1

Sageing 4

Nutmegging 5

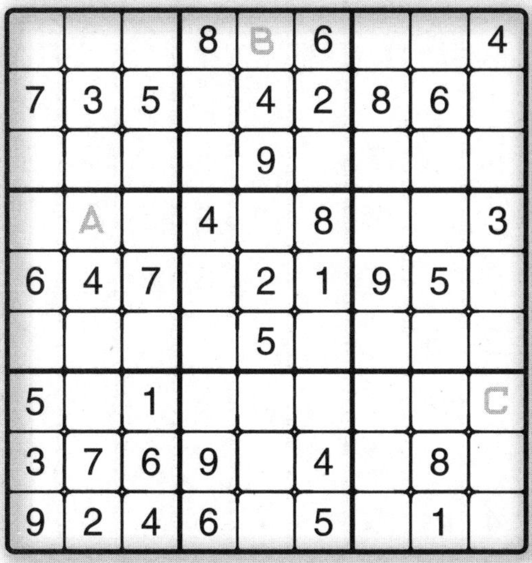

A Tom Baker, Sylvestor McCoy and Peter Davison have all played which character on television?

Sherlock Holmes	**1**
Blackadder	**9**
Doctor Who	**5**

B The 1958 film *A Night to Remember* depicts the first and last voyage of which ship?

Titanic	**7**
Queen Mary	***3***
Marie Celeste	**1**

C In 2004 the new Scottish Parliament building opened its doors in which city?

Edinburgh	**6**
Glasgow	**2**
Dundee	**9**

4

apprentice

	6		3	1	8	2		
A			7		9			
	3	7			2	9		8
	8	6		9	3			
9		1		B		3		
2	5			4		6	7	
				8				C
		8				4		
4		5		7	6		9	

A In Greek mythology, who was said to have the golden touch?

Ulysses	**5**
Midas	**8**
Medusa	**1**

B The nuts of the horse chestnut tree are commonly known as what?

Acorns	**6**
Conkers	**2**
Macadamias	**5**

C Which Biblical giant came from the city of Gath?

Samson	**3**
Magog	**7**
Goliath	**6**

	6	9	4	2				
7	2			5	3	4		6
3					6	7		9
	7		B	4		5		3
6		A			1			
	3			9			C	
	8			7		9	4	1
	1			6		2		8
	4			8		6	5	7

A What colour are the fifty stars on the US flag?

Red	**4**
White	**5**
Blue	**2**

B In which city is Lime Street the main railway terminus?

Liverpool	**6**
Birmingham	**2**
Manchester	**8**

C What does an insomniac find it difficult to do?

Relax	**1**
Swallow	**7**
Sleep	**6**

6

apprentice

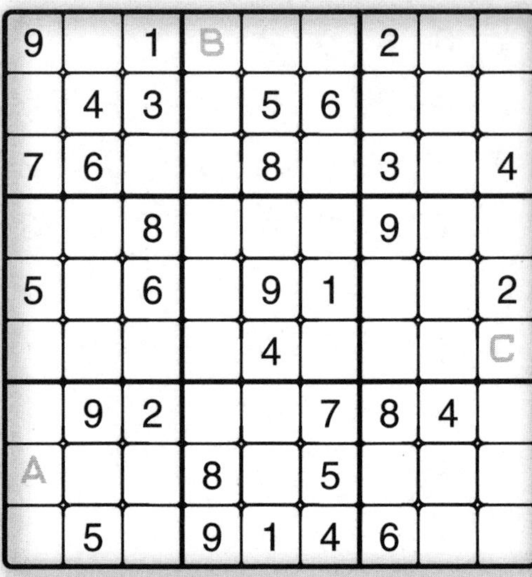

9
1
B
2
4
3
5
6
7
6
8
3
4
8
9
5
6
9
1
2
4
C
9
2
7
8
4
A
8
5
5
9
1
4
6

A Marrowfat is a variety of which vegetable?

Pea	**6**
Bean	**1**
Potato	**3**

B Which former Spice Girl had her second solo number-one hit in August 2000 with the dance track 'I Turn to You'?

Victoria Beckham	**3**
Geri Halliwell	**7**
Melanie Chisholm	**4**

C Which Dutch cheese is made in the shape of a large ball, normally sold with a red wax coating?

Edam	**1**
Gouda	**8**
Jarlsberg	**6**

7

apprentice

9	3	8	5			7		
1		7			B			
		2	1		8	9		6
			6				9	3
	7	5				8		4
	1		4	8		5	2	
	9	3		6			7	5
	8						C	
A			9					1

A The Ryder Cup is a major trophy in which sport?

Tennis 5

Golf 7

Baseball 6

B Who wrote the horror novels *Carrie* and *The Shining*, both of which have been made into films?

Edgar Allan Poe 4

Stephen King 2

H. P. Lovecraft 9

C Which city in the US is nicknamed the Windy City?

Chicago 4

San Francisco 3

New York 6

8

apprentice

A What began in Pudding Lane on 2 September 1666?

The Great Fire of London	**2**
The Plague	**7**
Printing	**9**

B Which word can mean cooking eggs, or the illicit catching of fish or game?

Scrambling	**1**
Coddling	**4**
Poaching	**8**

C *Hannibal* by Thomas Harris is the sequel to which novel?

Red Dragon	**4**
Black Sunday	**9**
The Silence of the Lambs	**3**

9 apprentice

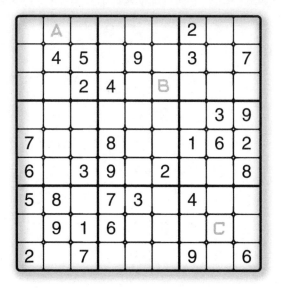

	A					2		
	4	5		9		3		7
		2	4		B			
							3	9
7			8			1	6	2
6		3	9		2			8
5	8		7	3		4		
	9	1	6				C	
2		7				9		6

A Stalactites are naturally formed mineral columns found in caves, but in which direction do they grow?

Upwards 1

Downwards 6

Sideways 7

B What name is given to the wars fought in England from 1455 to 1485, between the Houses of Lancaster and York?

The Northern Wars 3

The Shire Wars 5

The Wars of the Roses 8

C Which sea creature has a name that comes from the Greek words for 'eight' and 'foot'?

Octopus 7

Squid 2

Barnacle 8

10

apprentice

	4	6		2	9	3		
			B			8		4
	7				8	6	1	9
6	5		3		7		4	
				5	6	7	8	
	2		9	1				
A							6	
2			8	7		1	9	
	9			4				C

A Which singer was nicknamed Old Blue Eyes?

Frank Sinatra 1

Bing Crosby 8

Dean Martin 3

B Which New York park lies between Fifth and Eighth Avenue?

Madison Park 6

Prospect Park 5

Central Park 7

C In sport, what were held in Oslo in 1952 and in Lillehammer in 1994?

The Winter Olympic Games 8

The Commonwealth Games 2

The European Games 5

11

apprentice

9	2		B					
4	7		5	9			3	6
5	1				3	2		
2	3		9	5			4	7
				2	6	3		1
		4		1			C	8
				3	9	8		5
				8	4	9		2
8	6	A						

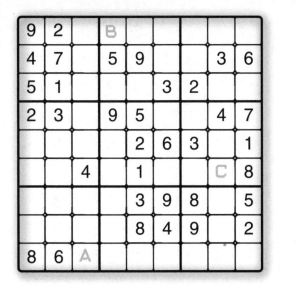

A Captain John Yossarian is the protagonist of which 1961 novel by American author Joseph Heller?

One Flew over the Cuckoo's Nest **1**

The Crying of Lot 49 **3**

Catch-22 **9**

B Which comedy actress plays the rebellious teenager Lauren, who has the catchphrase, 'Am I bovvered'?

Catherine Tate **8**

Ronnie Ancona **4**

Dawn French **7**

C Which country occupies the eastern half of the Scandinavian Peninsula?

Sweden **2**

Norway **5**

Finland **6**

12

apprentice

3	7			5	9	1	6	
		9	1			C		4
		1	B	3	2			9
2		4		6	1		3	5
1		3		7	4		2	8
	5	A				9		
8	6			9	5	4	1	
		5	3					6
		2		1	8			7

A Bankside Power Station in London re-opened in May 2000 as which art gallery?

The Hayward Gallery **7**

The National Portrait Gallery **8**

Tate Modern **6**

B Which Canadian city is served by Pierre Elliott Trudeau International Airport?

Montreal **7**

Ottawa **4**

Toronto **8**

C *Dazzler* is the autobiography of which England cricketer?

Graham Thorpe **2**

Darren Gough **3**

Michael Vaughan **5**

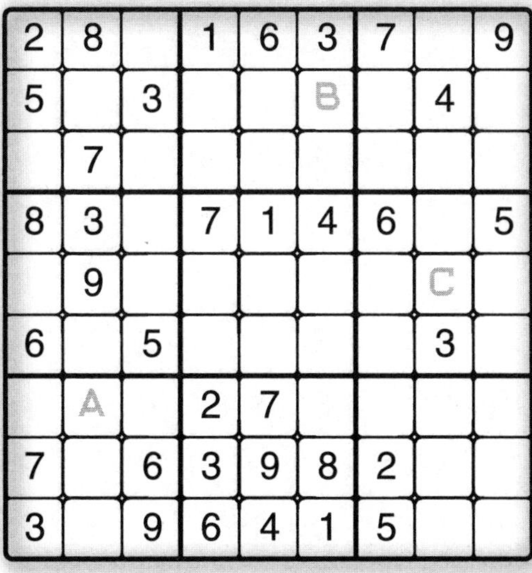

13

apprentice

A Who played the character Bren in the BBC sitcom *Dinnerladies*?

Victoria Wood	**4**
Julie Walters	**1**
Celia Imrie	**5**

B What do the lachrymal glands produce?

Sweat	**9**
Blood	**2**
Tears	**7**

C Who was the last monarch of the House of Tudor?

Henry VIII	**7**
Elizabeth I	**2**
Richard III	**8**

14

apprentice

	3		7	9	6	2		
	8		2	4		7		
	2		3	8	1	6		
7		A					8	
	9				B	5		
	6		5	1		3		
5	1		8	6		4	3	
	4	6				8		9
8			9	3			5	C

A Which composer wrote the scores for *ET*, *Jaws* and *Schindler's List*?

John Williams **4**

Michael Nyman **1**

John Barry **3**

B What does the acronym NATO stand for?

North Atlantic Treaty Organization **8**

National Act of Territory Orders **2**

New Artillery Treasury Office **4**

C In which sport have Andy Fordham, Phil Taylor and Ritchie Burnett all been world champions?

Snooker **1**

Curling **7**

Darts **6**

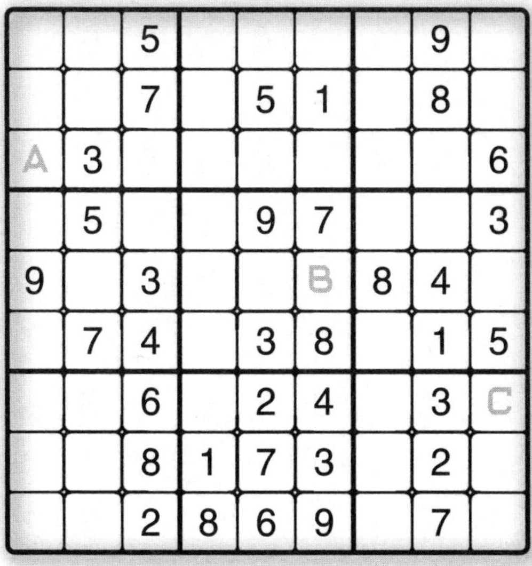

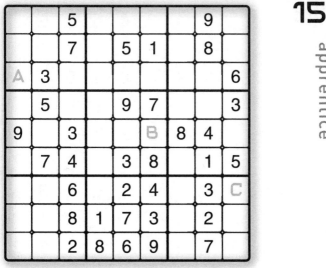

A Who played the role of Axel Foley in the *Beverley Hills Cop* series of films?

Eddie Murphy **1**

Leslie Nielsen **4**

Bruce Willis **8**

B Which international airport is linked to London by the M23 motorway?

Heathrow **2**

Luton **6**

Gatwick **5**

C Historically, sailors at sea who ate little fresh food suffered from scurvy. A lack of which vitamin causes this condition?

Vitamin E **1**

Vitamin C **8**

Vitamin A **9**

16

apprentice

		1		4		9	5	
	6		7	9		2		
	9	A			8	6		
9		7				8		C
	8			2	7		1	
1			5					7
3			2	1	6			
	7		9				4	
		6			B			2

A Amir Khan was an Olympic silver medallist in which sport?

Weightlifting 2

Wrestling 3

Boxing 5

B What is the nationality of the pop group The Cardigans?

Swedish 4

Polish 3

Spanish 5

C Which poet's work includes *Paradise Lost* and *Paradise Regained*?

John Milton 3

William Wordsworth 4

John Keats 6

17

apprentice

	A		7	9				
	8	9		3			7	5
		3	5	8	1			6
					8	C		
9				6	7	2	4	
		2					8	
				5	9		6	8
		5	B			9	1	
7		6			2	3		4

A What is the hardest part of the human body?

The toenails **4**

The skull **6**

Tooth enamel **1**

B Which Moroccan city's name means 'white house' in Spanish?

Casablanca **6**

Marrakech **3**

Rabat **8**

C In which English county would you find Leeds Castle?

Yorkshire **1**

Derbyshire **7**

Kent **5**

18

apprentice

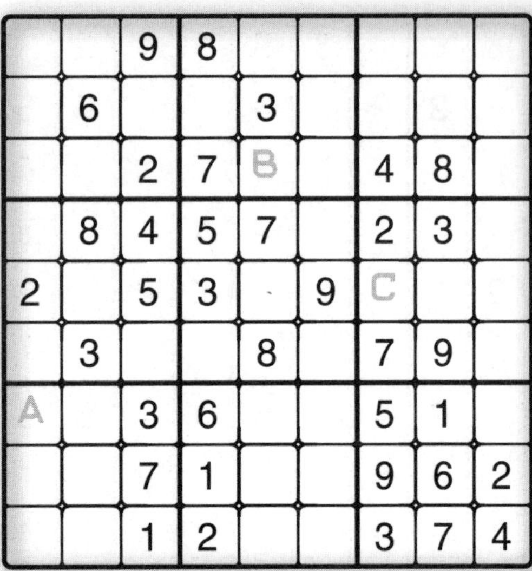

A What type of creature is a John Dory?

A snake	**8**
A fish	**4**
A bear	**9**

B Which international rugby team did Graham Henry coach before New Zealand?

England	**5**
Wales	**6**
Scotland	**9**

C $E=mc^2$ is part of which famous scientist's theories of relativity?

Isaac Newton	**1**
Albert Einstein	**8**
Edwin Hubble	**6**

6			5	8		7	2	
4	2						5	8
		A		3		9		1
				9				6
9	1		3			4		2
5							C	
	7			6	5		9	3
	4	6			B			
1	5	9		2			4	

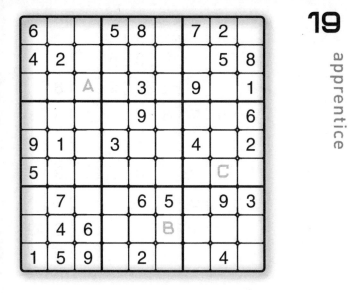

A Which Premiership football club's home ground is Fratton Park?

Portsmouth **5**

Southampton **7**

Port Vale **8**

B If someone suffers from bibliophobia, what are they afraid of?

Libraries **1**

Words **3**

Books **7**

C Which chemical element is known as plumbum and has the symbol Pb?

Lead **3**

Tin **1**

Platinum **7**

apprentice

	A					5		
4			8	3	6		1	
7			2	5	9		6	
	9	7	6					1
				1	B		5	
	6	2		4		7	3	8
	5	9	1					4
	7	1		9		8	2	6
				2			9	C

A Howard Shore composed the score for which fantasy trilogy?

Star Wars **1**

The Lord of the Rings **3**

Indiana Jones **8**

B Which *Friends* actress appeared in the video for Bruce Springsteen's 'Dancing in the Dark'?

Courteney Cox **2**

Jennifer Aniston **3**

Lisa Kudrow **7**

C Espanyol is the lesser-known football club in which Spanish city?

Madrid **3**

Barcelona **5**

Bilbao **7**

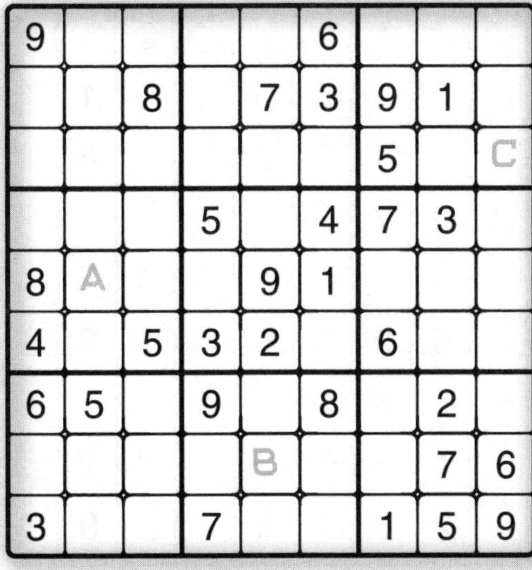

21

apprentice

A Which presenter of the current BBC series *Strictly Come Dancing* is famous for the catchphrase, 'Nice to see you, to see you ... nice!'?

Jimmy Savile 2

Graham Norton 6

Bruce Forsyth 7

B *Forty Licks* was the title of the 2002 greatest hits album by which sixties rock band?

The Who 1

The Rolling Stones 3

Cream 4

C In golf, who is the youngest-ever winner of the US Masters?

Tiger Woods 2

Seve Ballesteros 3

Nick Faldo 8

22

apprentice

7		1	8			2	5	9
9		5	3			6	7	4
	A						8	1
3		7			5			
	9					C		
	5	2	7	3		4	1	6
5		3			4			
	1		B					
	2	8	1	9		5	6	7

A George Lucas received Academy award nominations for directing and writing which 1977 science fiction film?

2001: A Space Odyssey **3**
Alien **6**
Star Wars **4**

B The Oliver Stone film *Platoon* is set during which twentieth-century conflict?

The Vietnam War **5**
The Korean War **2**
The Cuban Missile Crisis **3**

C Which children's television character has a cat named Pilchard?

Postman Pat **3**
Bob the Builder **7**
Fireman Sam **8**

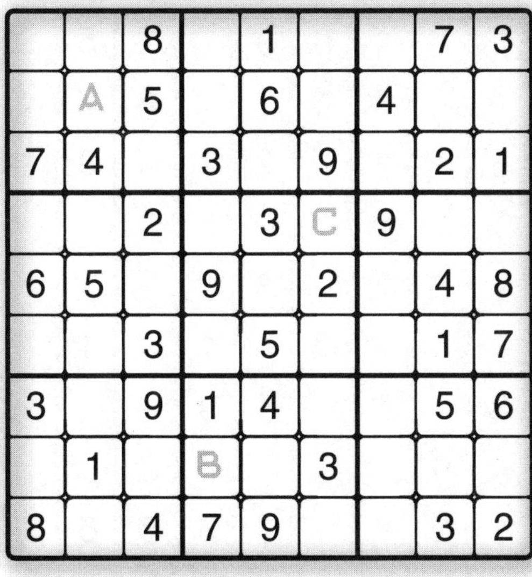

23

apprentice

		8		1			7	3
	A	5		6		4		
7	4		3		9		2	1
		2		3	C	9		
6	5		9		2		4	8
		3		5			1	7
3		9	1	4			5	6
	1		B		3			
8		4	7	9			3	2

A Which television comedy series features characters called Mr Cheque Please and Skipinder the Punjabi Kangaroo?

Goodness Gracious Me **3**

The Fast Show **2**

Coupling **9**

B Who topped the album and singles charts in July 2005 with *Back to Bedlam* and 'You're Beautiful' respectively?

James Blunt **6**

Will Young **2**

Richard Ashcroft **5**

C Which epic nineteenth-century novel by Leo Tolstoy is set during the Napoleonic Wars?

Anna Karenina **4**

The Kingdom of God is Within You **8**

War and Peace **1**

24

apprentice

	A		6	9				
		3	5	1	4	2		
6		5		2		9		1
1						8		
7	8			3	6		9	
			B		1			
3		1		5	9			C
4	9					5		
	2	7			8	3	6	

A Which British prime minister is the only one to have also held the three great offices of state: home secretary, foreign secretary and chancellor of the exchequer?

Winston Churchill **4**

James Callaghan **1**

Margaret Thatcher **7**

B Which French king was guillotined in 1793?

Louis XVI **4**

Louis XV **2**

Louis XIV **9**

C Scoter and mandarin are members of which family of birds?

Duck **8**

Parrot **4**

Swan **7**

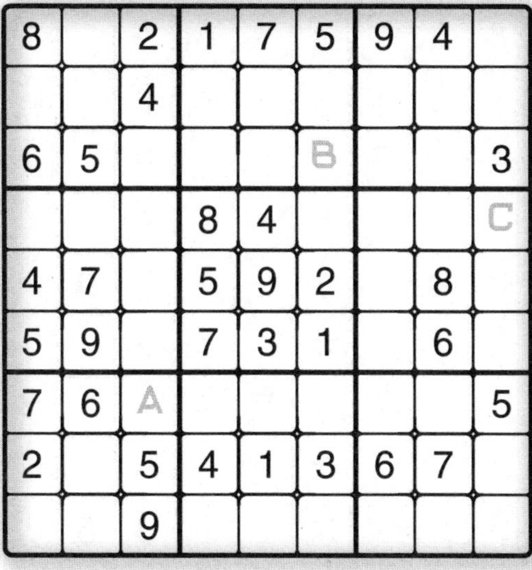

25

apprentice

A Which marsupial has fingerprints so similar to the human fingerprint that it is almost impossible to tell them apart?

The kangaroo	**3**
The koala	**1**
The wombat	**8**

B In 2004 'Do They Know It's Christmas' was the Christmas number one, but in which year was it first number one?

1984	**4**
1983	**8**
1987	**9**

C Which mountain in Southern Italy is the only active volcano on mainland Europe, and last erupted in 1944?

Mount Etna	**1**
Mount Rushmore	**2**
Mount Vesuvius	**7**

26

apprentice

8	6			7	5		C	
	5	1		2		8		6
4		9				3		
		A	2		7			
3	9				1	2	6	
	7		9	4	6	5		
5		7		9	4			3
				6				
2			B			9		

A 0151 is the dialling code for which British city?

Liverpool **5**
Sheffield **4**
Edinburgh **8**

B What would be your star sign if you were born on Christmas Day?

Capricorn **7**
Sagittarius **1**
Aquarius **3**

C Into which sea do the English rivers the Tyne, Tees and Humber flow?

The Irish Sea **2**
The Baltic Sea **4**
The North Sea **9**

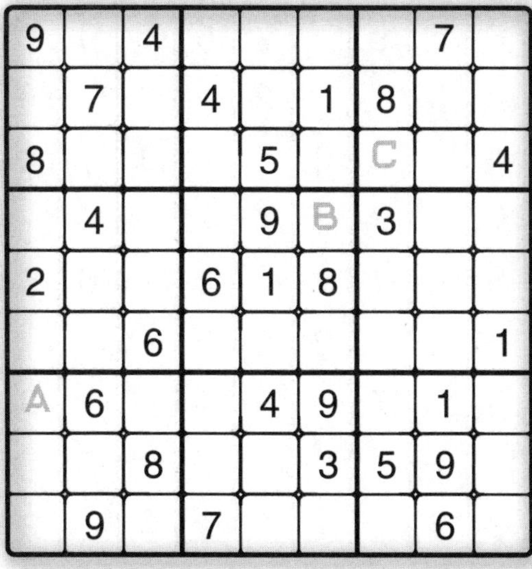

A In the human body, what is the common name of the joint between the humerus in the upper arm, and the radius and the ulna in the lower arm?

The wrist **5**

The collarbone **7**

The elbow **3**

B What is the name of the aria performed by Luciano Pavarotti and used as a theme to the 1990 World Cup?

'Ave Maria' **2**

'Three Lions' **7**

'Nessun Dorma' **5**

C Who starred as Susan in the film *Desperately Seeking Susan*?

Madonna **6**

Cher **1**

Whitney Houston **9**

28

apprentice

A		8			5		9	
1				3				
			6			4	1	3
5			4				7	
		4			2	1		5
	2		9	5			C	
	9	7		4		8		
	1				3	9	5	
	3		B		9			2

A In 2005, in which seaside resort in Essex was the world's longest pier damaged by fire that destroyed its arcade?

Southend on Sea 3

Canvey Island 2

Harwich 7

B The elderly Andalusian duo, Los del Rio, recorded which 1996 Euro dance-craze single?

'Saturday Night' 5

'The Locomotion' 8

'Macarena' 1

C In which film does James Bond kill his adversary Hugo Drax with a poisonous dart from his wristwatch?

Moonraker 8

The Spy Who Loved Me 3

Goldeneye 4

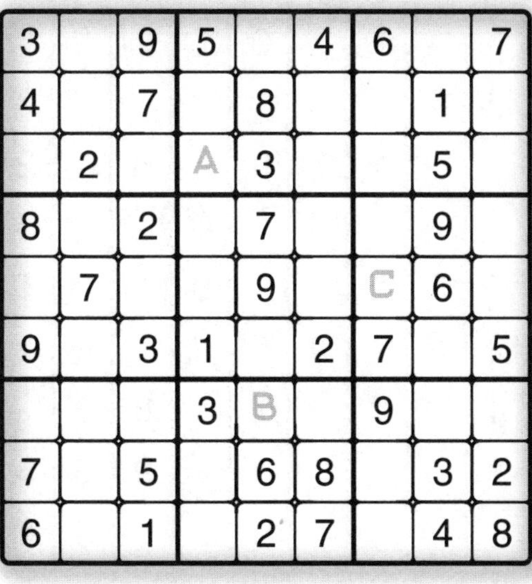

29

apprentice

A Who had a UK number-three hit in 1978 with the theme song from the film *Grease*?

John Travolta	**6**
The Bee Gees	**9**
Frankie Valli	**7**

B Which writer created the Earl of Emsworth, who lived at Blandings Castle?

P. G. Wodehouse	**5**
Jerome K. Jerome	**1**
Oscar Wilde	**4**

C On the London Underground map what colour is used to represent the Central Line?

Red	**2**
Yellow	**1**
Pink	**3**

30

apprentice

				3				
9	A							7
		1		9	5	6		2
			7		6	C		
7	3				8		9	1
2			9	5	3		6	
4		3		7		8	2	
1			B			9		5
				6	2		3	4

A Who won the 1961 Pulitzer Prize for her novel *To Kill a Mockingbird*?

Iris Murdoch 2

Harper Lee 4

Naomi Wolf 8

B Anne Bancroft and Dustin Hoffman starred in which film that featured songs by Simon and Garfunkel?

Cabaret 4

The Graduate 3

Bonnie and Clyde 8

C In 1991, which Canadian singer spent a record 16 consecutive weeks at number one in the UK singles chart?

Shania Twain 3

Bryan Adams 2

Celine Dion 5

Round Two

1

warrior

		5		8	4	3		
4					B		1	
	2			3	1			8
7	4		9				3	2
5	3		7				9	1
				5	8		C	
8	A						2	
		2		9	3	4		
	9			2	7			6

A Which war, despite its name, actually lasted approximately 115 years?

The Ten Years War **1**

The Twenty Years War **5**

The Hundred Years War **7**

B In the *Fawlty Towers* episode 'Gourmet Night' Basil Fawlty gave his car a 'damn good thrashing' with what?

A whip **6**

A rolling pin **2**

A tree branch **9**

C The BCG vaccine is given to protect against which disease?

Tuberculosis **6**

Measles **7**

Polio **4**

2

warrior

5	6	8		2		9		
7	2			4	6			
4		9					6	C
			4	7	3			
	3		8		9		7	5
	B	7		5	2			
		1	3			6		8
					5	2	9	
A		5					1	

A The name of which flesh-eating dinosaur comes from the Greek and Latin combination for 'tyrant lizard king'?

Velociraptor 2

Tyrannosaurus Rex 6

Allosaurus 3

B In 1967 Engelbert Humperdinck went to number one in the UK with 'Release Me', preventing which famous band from attaining their twelfth successive chart-topper?

The Beatles 4

The Rolling Stones 1

The Who 8

C In which county is Sandringham House?

Berkshire 1

Norfolk 2

Buckinghamshire 3

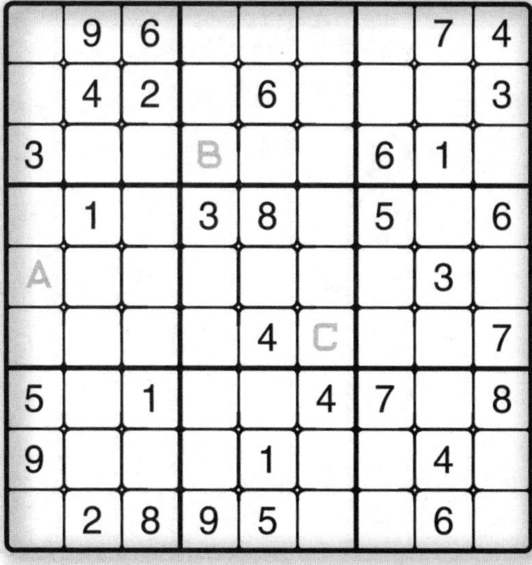

3

warrior

A What completes the proverb, 'A watched pot...'?

Never boils 6

Cooks the best 2

Spoils the broth 4

B Which twentieth-century music icon's middle name was Aaron?

Johnny Cash 2

Ray Charles 7

Elvis Presley 4

C Who has played Pauline Fowler since the first episode of *EastEnders*?

Wendy Richard 5

Letitia Dean 3

Gillian Taylforth 1

4

warrior

			9		3			8
	1		4	8	5	9		
	3	8		1	6			
A		5				1		9
2			7			8	4	
			5	B				7
3	6	2					C	
	5	1	6					
4		9		2			5	6

A Which British rower won a gold medal at five consecutive Olympic Games?

Steve Redgrave **8**

James Cracknell **6**

Matthew Pinsent **7**

B Amity Island is the setting for which blockbuster movie?

Jaws **9**

Jurassic Park **4**

The Beach **3**

C In the Christian calendar, what name is given to the day before Ash Wednesday?

Easter Tuesday **1**

Whit Tuesday **7**

Shrove Tuesday **9**

5 warrior

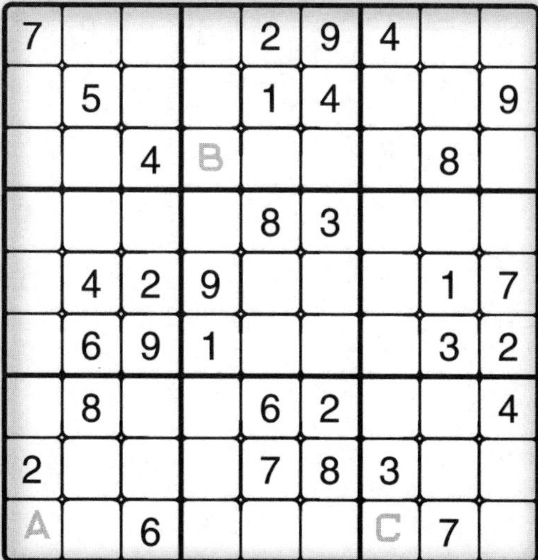

A Which 1990s television series starring Catherine Zeta-Jones and Pam Ferris was based on a series of novels by H. E. Bates?

Prisoner Cell Block H	**1**
The Darling Buds of May	**4**
Birds of a Feather	**9**

B Which boxer played himself in the film *The Greatest*?

Muhammad Ali	**7**
Joe Frazier	**3**
Mike Tyson	**5**

C In which television series can you find the Nag's Head pub?

Open All Hours	**1**
Steptoe and Son	**9**
Only Fools and Horses	**2**

6

warrior

A The seismograph was originally designed to record the intensity of which natural phenomenon?

Floods	**8**
Earthquakes	**1**
Tornados	**6**

B What breed of dog is Scooby-Doo?

Great Dane	**5**
Sheepdog	**4**
Alsatian	**8**

C Who starred as the exotic dancer Satine in the 2001 film *Moulin Rouge*?

Demi Moore	**2**
Sharon Stone	**3**
Nicole Kidman	**9**

7
warrior

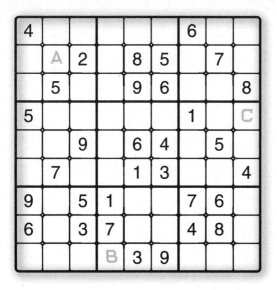

4						6		
	A	2		8	5		7	
	5			9	6			8
5						1		C
		9		6	4		5	
	7			1	3			4
9		5	1			7	6	
6		3	7			4	8	
			B	3	9			

A What colour does litmus paper turn in alkaline solutions?

Blue **6**
Green **1**
Yellow **3**

B Red, English and Gordon are all breeds of which type of gundog?

Setter **6**
Terrier **2**
Spaniel **4**

C In the Old Testament, what was the name of the first son of Adam and Eve, who slew his brother Abel?

Cain **6**
Abraham **3**
Noah **7**

8

warrior

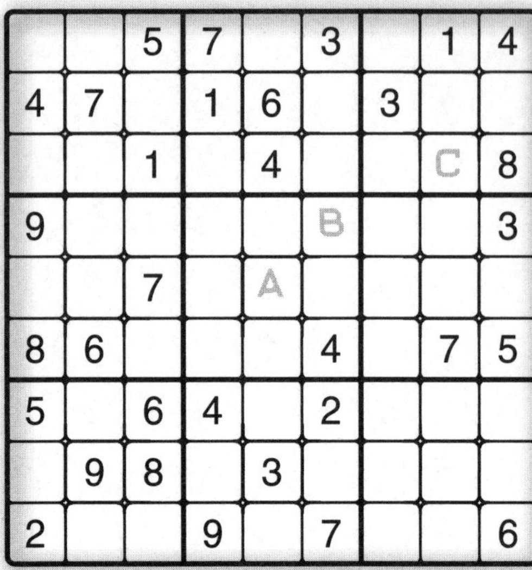

A Where in London do the Wombles live?

Hampstead Heath	**8**
Hyde Park	**9**
Wimbledon Common	**5**

B In the film *The Wizard of Oz*, what did the Tin Man wear as a hat?

A funnel	**1**
A bucket	**5**
A watering can	**8**

C Which of the Great Lakes of North America shares its name with the state in which Detroit can be found?

Lake Erie	**9**
Lake Michigan	**6**
Lake Ontario	**2**

			4	7				8
	1	5			8	6		
8	4				3		1	
		B		3				1
A			1				7	
			5	2	7		9	3
	3						2	4
	5	1				7		
9	6				C	3		

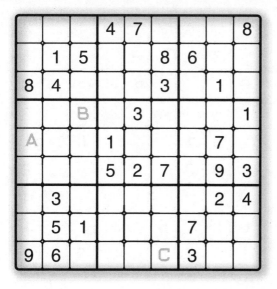

A Which Welsh singer sang with Cerys Matthews on a 1999 version of the old standard 'Baby, It's Cold Outside'?

Charlotte Church 6

Shirley Bassey 3

Tom Jones 5

B The Oscar-winning song 'Talk to the Animals', comes from which 1967 film?

Doctor Dolittle 9

The Jungle Book 2

The Lion King 4

C Who became the first England footballer to be sent off twice in internationals, the second time being in 2005?

Alan Shearer 1

Michael Owen 4

David Beckham 2

10

warrior

		4	3		6	1		
	3			B				8
6			8		4		2	
			4		2			
	6	1		9		8		5
	9	3		5		6		2
A	1						C	4
8			6		9		1	
		7	5		1	9		

A What colour are the seats in the House of Lords?

Red 9

Green 5

Blue 2

B What is a more common name for the patella?

The collarbone 1

The elbow 2

The kneecap 7

C In which city would you find the international sports venue Murrayfield?

Cardiff 7

Edinburgh 3

Manchester 8

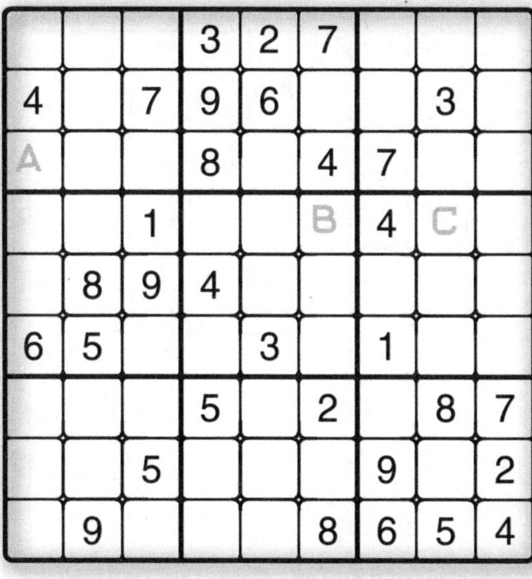

A On the Pathfinder series of Ordnance Survey maps, the letters PC stand for what?

Portcullis	**2**
Private campsite	**9**
Public convenience	**5**

B The Torah is a name given to the sacred writings of which religion?

Judaism	**6**
Christianity	**3**
Islam	**9**

C Which Pop Idol recently made his film debut in *Mrs Henderson Presents*?

Will Young	**9**
Gareth Gates	**7**
Darius Danesh	**6**

12

warrior

	1						B	8
9				3	5	1		
		2		8	6		5	
	5	A						3
		1		9	3		4	
7				4	1	2		
1	9		8			3		2
6	3		2			4		5
				6	9		C	

A In literature, whose address was 'The Cupboard under the Stairs, Number Four, Privet Drive'?

Peter Pan	**4**
Harry Potter	**9**
Bilbo Baggins	**7**

B Braunschweiger, beer sticks and bratwurst are forms of which food?

Sausage	**3**
Bread	**2**
Apple	**6**

C Which dramatist and poet is said to have been born on 23 April 1564, and died on the same date in 1616?

Geoffrey Chaucer	**8**
John Milton	**1**
William Shakespeare	**7**

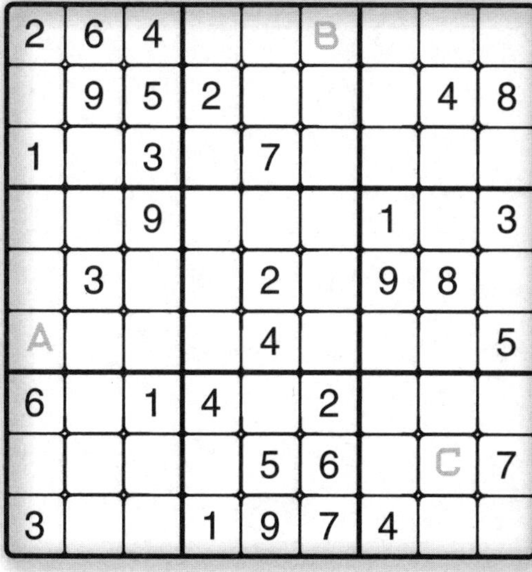

13

warrior

A *Starry Night* and *Sunflowers* are works by which Dutch artist?

Vincent van Gogh	**8**
Rembrandt	**7**
Pieter de Hooch	**9**

B Which sport do the San Antonio Spurs play?

Baseball	**1**
Basketball	**5**
Ice hockey	**3**

C Which organization has the motto, 'Nation shall speak peace unto nation'?

The BBC	**1**
The United Nations	**2**
The World Health Organization	**3**

14

warrior

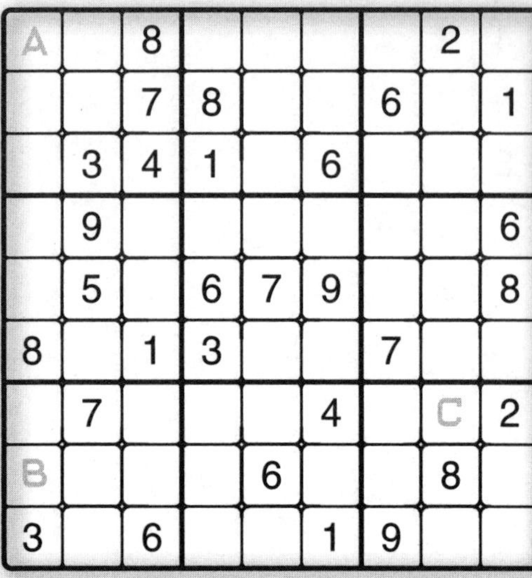

A What name is shared by the hero of a Robert Burns poem and a kind of hat?

Tam o'Shanter	**6**
Jim O'Connor	**1**
Jock Bowler	**5**

B What word links a colour, a fruit, a Dutch royal house and a South African river?

Orange	**2**
Lemon	**4**
Plum	**9**

C Which chemical element has the symbol I?

Iron	**9**
Iodine	**6**
Iridium	**5**

15

warrior

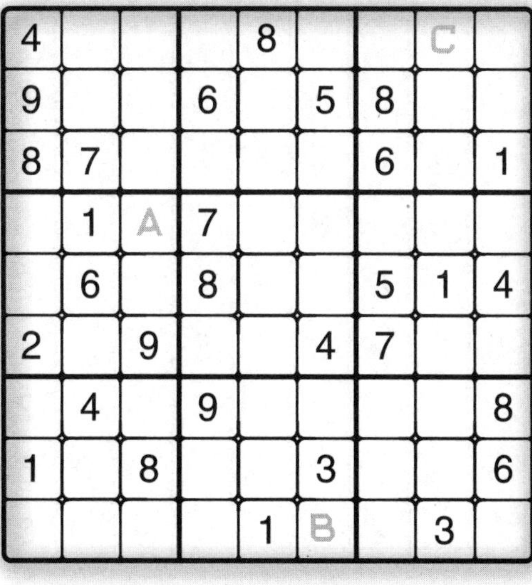

A Which nineties rock group took its name from a seventeenth-century English republican movement?

Primal Scream	**3**
The Charlatans	**5**
The Levellers	**4**

B If someone was to go and shop in a philatelists' shop, what would they be interested in buying?

Stamps	**8**
Hats	**2**
Coins	**7**

C Which British athlete has won 11 Paralympic gold medals in their career?

Matt Walker	**2**
Tanni Grey-Thompson	**9**
Liz Miller	**5**

16

warrior

6					1	7		5
		5			3		1	4
A	1		8	4				
	5		3					
		8		5			C	
	3	9	2	7	8			
8						5		7
3				B			9	6
	4	2						3

A What was the name of the ship on which scientist Charles Darwin travelled to the Pacific to research his theory of evolution?

Discovery **2**

Beagle **7**

Endeavour **9**

B Who is the acclaimed poet, critic and biographer who became Poet Laureate in 1999, succeeding Ted Hughes?

Andrew Motion **8**

John Betjeman **1**

Cecil Day-Lewis **2**

C Which member of the English World cup-winning squad coached the Ireland side that reached the 1990 and 1994 World Cup finals?

Jack Charlton **7**

Bobby Charlton **3**

Geoff Hurst **4**

17

warrior

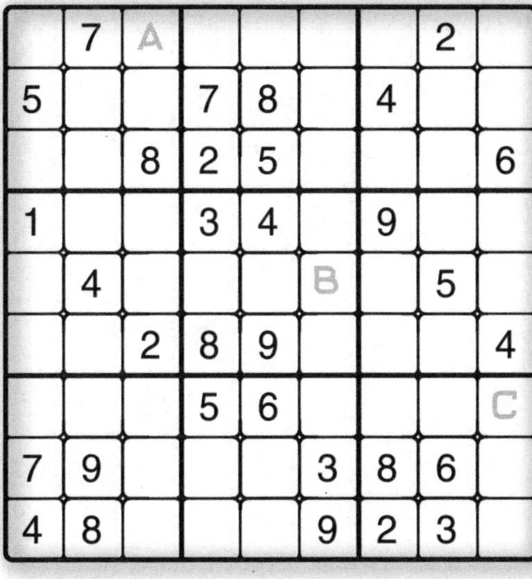

A Which city is known as Scotland's Granite City?

Aberdeen	**4**
Perth	**6**
Stirling	**9**

B What surname links singers Loretta, Tami and Vera?

Drake	**1**
Lynn	**2**
Wynette	**7**

C Edward Rochester and Bertha Mason are characters in which Charlotte Brontë novel?

Jane Eyre	**9**
Wuthering Heights	**1**
The Tenant of Wildfell Hall	**7**

18

warrior

	6		1		B			
	5	2	8		3		7	
				2				
	8		2				6	4
			6	1			9	8
				7	8	2	C	
6			5		1	3		7
A	7			6		9		
	3	9		8			4	5

A What is the capital city of Portugal?

Porto 1

Lisbon 8

Madrid 4

B Steve McQueen starred as Captain Virgil 'The Cooler King Hilts' in which 1963 film?

Bullitt 5

The Magnificent Seven 9

The Great Escape 7

C Which athlete won a double gold for Britain in the 2004 Athens Olympic Games?

Paula Radcliffe 1

Kelly Sotherton 5

Kelly Holmes 3

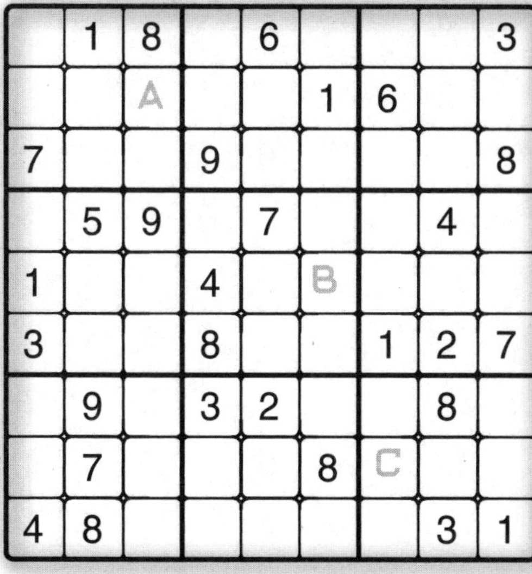

19

warrior

A The Battle of Waterloo took place in which country?

Luxembourg	**2**
Holland	**5**
Belgium	**4**

B 'Pants to Poverty' was the 2001 slogan for which charity?

Comic Relief	**6**
Band Aid	**3**
Shelter	**2**

C For what did the initials JR stand in JR Ewing of *Dallas* fame?

John Ross	**9**
John Robin	**4**
John Richard	**5**

20

warrior

		1	9	4				5
	8				B	1		
9			1	6			7	
4	3				6	9	2	
		A	3	8				
5	6				9	4	1	
	5					2		C
		3	8	5				4
1			4	2			8	

A Which London cathedral stands at the top of Ludgate Hill?

Westminster Abbey 2

Southwark 7

St Paul's 9

B In which American state will you find the Grand Canyon?

Arizona 5

Nevada 2

California 3

C Geena Davies, Susan Sarandon and a young Brad Pitt starred in which 1991 film?

Mermaids 6

Single White Female 9

Thelma & Louise 1

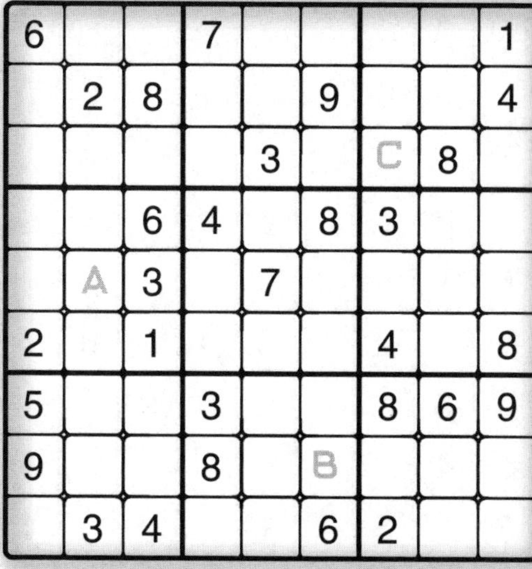

A Which influential designer launched his revolutionary tuxedo jacket for women in 1966?

Giorgio Armani **5**

Calvin Klein **9**

Yves Saint Laurent **8**

B In chess, what is another name for the castle?

The fortress **2**

The keep **4**

The rook **1**

C Which aquatic mammal lives in a den known as a holt?

The beaver **5**

The otter **6**

The water rat **7**

22

warrior

	2				B			
7		8			1	2	5	
A		3					4	
	3	4		8	9			
8	1		2					
		2		6	4		8	
	8			5	6	9	7	
	4		9				1	C
3		5	7	1				4

A Who was the first English king of the House of Lancaster?

Henry IV	**1**
Henry II	**5**
Henry I	**6**

B In which country were the first three cricket World Cup competitions held?

England	**5**
India	**3**
Australia	**7**

C Who wrote the Richard Sharpe novels set in the Napoleonic wars?

Winston Graham	**2**
Catherine Cookson	**6**
Bernard Cornwell	**8**

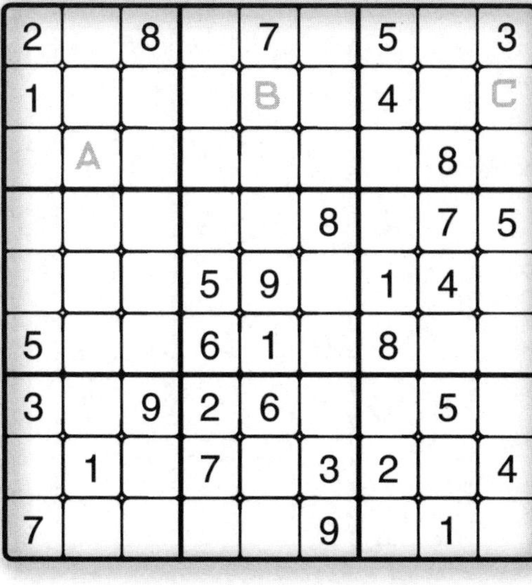

23

warrior

A The capital of the state of North Carolina is named after which Englishman?

Sir Walter Scott	**7**
Sir Walter Raleigh	**6**
Sir Francis Drake	**9**

B How many times did Martina Navratilova win the ladies' singles title at Wimbledon?

Eight	**2**
Nine	**8**
Ten	**5**

C In the Bible, who was robbed of his strength when Delilah cut his hair?

Samson	**7**
Isaac	**6**
Abraham	**9**

24

warrior

8				9	5	7		1
	7	3						
9				1	4	8	C	6
	4	8			2			9
			B	4		3		
	9	1	6				4	
	3	6	1				7	
A				5		6		
	1	5			3			4

A What does the 'W' stand for in George W. Bush?

Walker 2

William 4

Westfield 7

B The ruins of Tintern Abbey stand by which river?

The Tyne 5

The Thames 8

The Wye 9

C The name of which reptile is thought to come from the Spanish for 'the lizard'?

Alligator 3

Crocodile 2

Iguana 5

25

warrior

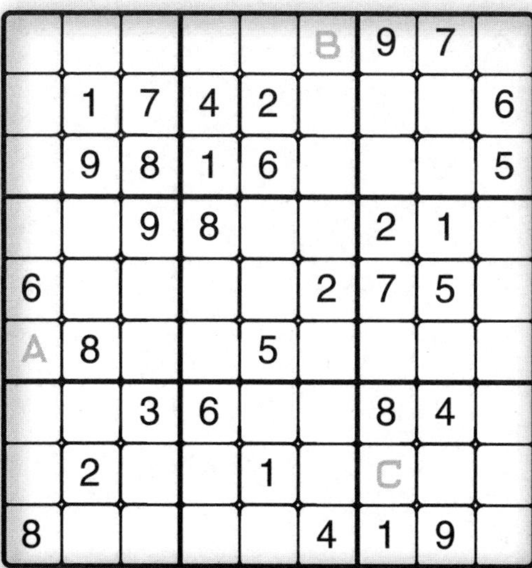

A Which American president was portrayed by Antony Hopkins in a 1995 film?

Abraham Lincoln	**1**
George Bush	**7**
Richard Nixon	**4**

B George Orwell wrote about the road to which pier?

Brighton Pier	**5**
Pier 39	**8**
Wigan Pier	**3**

C Which famous residence has the postcode SW1A 2AA?

10 Downing Street	**5**
221b Baker Street	**3**
Buckingham Palace	**6**

26

warrior

4	A							7
		1		2	4		9	
	3			6	9	4		
9		8	2				6	5
6		4	9				3	2
				7	5			
	6			3	7	5		C
		7		8	6		4	
8			B					3

A Which Scottish football team play at Ibrox Park?

Celtic 5

Rangers 9

Dundee United 8

B Which comedian had 19 UK chart entries between 1960 and 1981, all of them romantic ballads?

Harry Secombe 1

Tommy Trinder 4

Ken Dodd 5

C Sofia Coppola's 2003 film *Lost in Translation* was set in which city?

New York 1

Paris 9

Tokyo 8

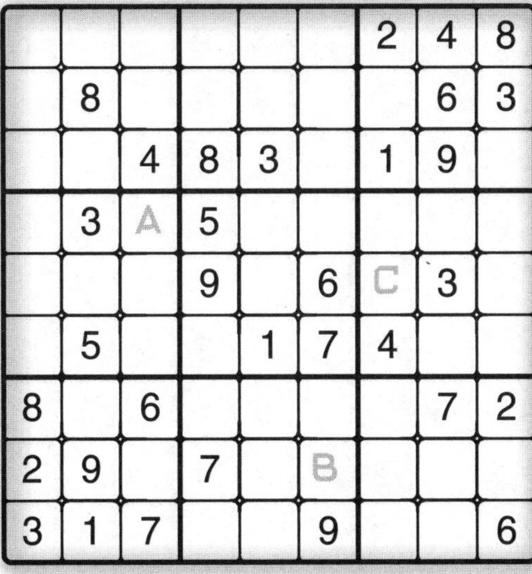

27

warrior

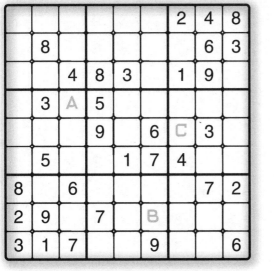

A Poseidon, brother of Zeus and son of Cronus and Rhea, was god of which natural resource?

The air 2

The land 8

The sea 9

B In cricket, who captained England to the Ashes victory in 2005?

Michael Vaughan 8

Marcus Trescothick 1

Andrew Flintoff 5

C *Manhattan and Mighty Aphrodite* are films by which New York-born writer and director?

Woody Allen 7

Martin Scorsese 5

Francis Ford Coppola 8

28

warrior

	4	2		3	9			6
			2	5	6			
	A		4		1		2	
9			1			4	3	7
		7				5	9	
			5		7	2		1
7	3			6			8	C
1		9			4			
		8		B			4	

A In Greek mythology, which woman was bestowed with special qualities by all the gods and goddesses?

Hera **5**

Diana **8**

Pandora **7**

B In the televison series *Porridge*, who shared a cell with Norman Stanley Fletcher?

MacKay **2**

Barrowclough **9**

Godber **1**

C In which athletic event would you perform a Fosbury flop?

The high jump **2**

The discus **5**

The javelin **9**

29

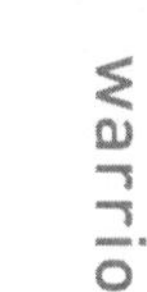

1	2	6		8	5			
		5			6			C
	9		B	3				
8			3			5	1	
7				5			9	4
	1	4			2			
				1	3		4	
	A		4			1	7	
			8				6	5

A There are four passport offices in England – in London, Liverpool, Durham and where else?

Peterborough	**5**
Dover	**3**
Newcastle	**8**

B Whose only appearance as James Bond came in the 1969 film *On Her Majesty's Secret Service*?

George Lazenby	**2**
David Niven	**1**
Timothy Dalton	**7**

C In which sport would you use a foil to compete?

Shooting	**2**
Fencing	**1**
Fishing	**9**

30

warrior

1	2				8		4	
	7	9		3				
	A	4					3	
			5	8	6			
			3	7			5	C
3		5		9	1			8
		2			B	6	9	
	9		7			3	1	2
			6	2		5		7

A Who wrote Lulu's 1974 hit 'The Man Who Sold the World'?

Lulu 5

Sir Paul McCartney 6

David Bowie 8

B *Animal Farm* was written by which author?

H. G. Wells 4

George Orwell 3

Rudyard Kipling 5

C Which actress and Dame plays the role of Professor Minerva McGonagall in the Harry Potter films?

Dame Judi Dench 1

Dame Maggie Smith 6

Dame Hilda Bracket 9

Round Three

1

shogun

		3		B			7	
7	8					6		3
9	4					1		5
A		1		9			8	
	9		1		5			6
5			7		6	4		
		5		6			9	
	6		8		3		C	1
8			9		1	3		

A Cardiology is branch of medicine that focuses on which area of the body?

The heart **6**

The lungs **4**

The liver **2**

B Fagin and the Artful Dodger are characters in which Charles Dickens novel?

David Copperfield **5**

Great Expectations **1**

Oliver Twist **2**

C Which composer wrote *The Four Seasons*?

Vivaldi **5**

Beethoven **4**

Mozart **2**

2 shogun

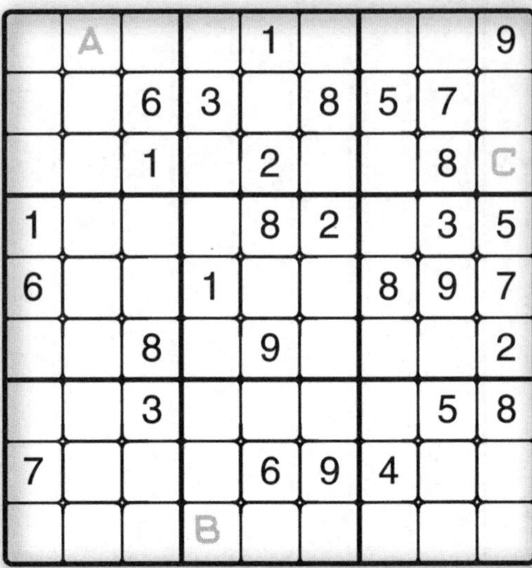

A 1 9
6 3 8 5 7
1 2 8 C
1 8 2 3 5
6 1 8 9 7
8 9 2
3 5 8
7 6 9 4
B

A Which novel by William Golding features a group of schoolboys stranded on a desert island, who become savages without adult supervision?

Lord of the Flies **3**

Tom Brown's Schooldays **8**

Treasure Island **4**

B Which successful boy band officially split on Valentine's Day 1996?

Westlife **2**

Take That **5**

Blue **7**

C Which annual sporting event takes place between Putney and Mortlake over a distance of 4 miles and 374 yards?

The London Marathon **3**

The Notting Hill Carnival **6**

The Boat Race **4**

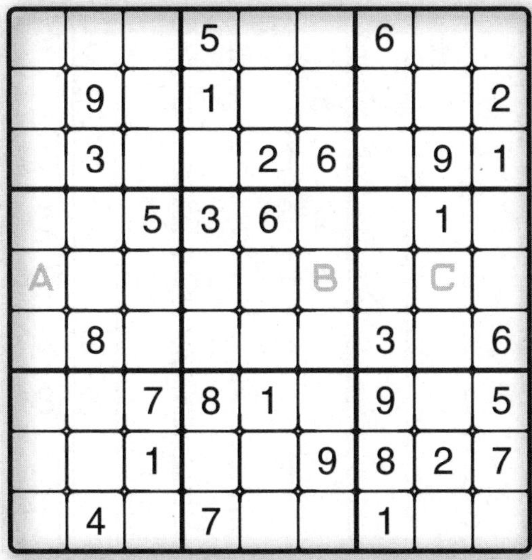

3

shogun

A In November 2000, which guitarist married Anita Dobson, who played Angie Watts in *EastEnders*?

Brian May 1

Eric Clapton 6

Bill Wyman 9

B Who played the role of Renton in the film *Trainspotting*?

Ewan McGregor 5

Robert Carlyle 2

Daniel Craig 8

C Which Hollywood star recently proposed to Katie Holmes at the top of the Eiffel Tower ?

Brad Pitt 4

Ben Affleck 8

Tom Cruise 7

4

shogun

	5			1			4	C
3		9	6			1		
6		2			7			9
			4		5	7		1
			9		6	3		4
	A			7			9	
	3			9	B		6	
7		4	5			2		
5		1			4			7

A What symbol of division finally fell on 9 November 1989?

Hadrian's Wall	**4**
The Berlin Wall	**8**
The Great Wall of China	**6**

B Which novel opens with the words, 'Marley was dead'?

A Christmas Carol	**1**
War and Peace	**2**
The Fall of the House of Usher	**8**

C Which gas has the chemical formula CO_2?

Carbon monoxide	**2**
Calcium carbide	**8**
Carbon dioxide	**3**

2					1	6		
	4	5	6	7				
	7	1					4	3
A					5		8	1
		9	4				7	
	3			B		2		
	1			5				6
			1	8		5		
		3			9			C

A In rugby union, how many points are scored for a converted try?

Seven **7**

Three **4**

Two **6**

B What is the name of the King of Spain?

King Ferdinand II **6**

King Alfonso III **9**

King Juan Carlos I **1**

C According to the saying: 'I' comes before 'E' except after which letter?

C **8**

D **2**

S **7**

6

shogun

A Which of Shakespeare's romantic heroines was married and had killed herself before her 14th birthday?

Cleopatra	**2**
Ophelia	**8**
Juliet	**5**

B In what year did Queen Elizabeth II accede to the throne?

1952	**4**
1951	**1**
1954	**8**

C 'Five Colours in Her Hair' was the first number-one hit of which boy band?

Busted	**4**
Five	**6**
McFly	**2**

7

shogun

8		5	7	9				
	9	A			3			
1		3	2	8				
		6		2		8	3	
3			8			1	2	C
	7				9			5
	8			B	1			2
9			3			6	7	
		1		7		9	5	

A What is the capital city of Argentina?

São Paulo 4

Rio de Janeiro 7

Buenos Aires 2

B A military rising headed by General Franco in 1936 led to civil war in which European country?

Spain 6

Italy 4

France 5

C Calcium carbonate is the chemical name for which writing material?

Chalk 7

Lead 6

Ink 9

A What was the name of Charlotte Church's first classical album?

Voice of an Angel	**6**
Voice of a Girl	**5**
Voice of a Saint	**8**

B Which superhero hails from Gotham city?

Batman	**8**
Spiderman	**1**
Superman	**2**

C What is the most common element in the universe?

Oxygen	**2**
Hydrogen	**7**
Nitrogen	**9**

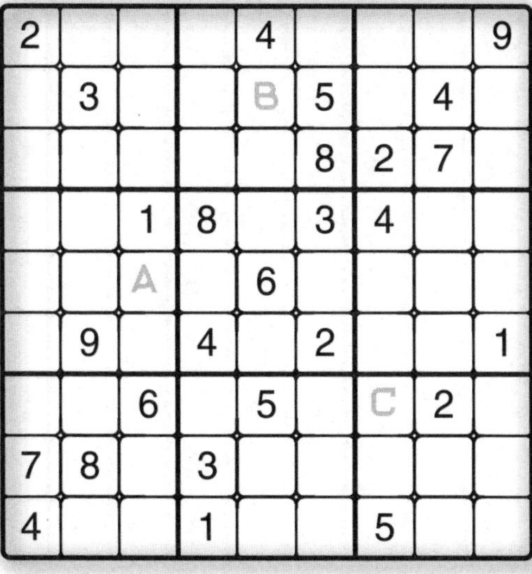

A *Fever Pitch* by Nick Hornby is about a supporter of which English football team?

Arsenal	**2**
Manchester United	**3**
Sheffield Wednesday	**5**

B What was the first creature to leave Noah's ark when it finally came to rest?

A giraffe	**7**
A cat	**9**
A raven	**1**

C Ken Kesey's 1962 novel set in a psychiatric ward was made into a 1975 film starring Jack Nicholson; what was it called?

The Shining	**1**
Five Easy Pieces	**8**
One Flew over the Cuckoo's Nest	**9**

10

shogun

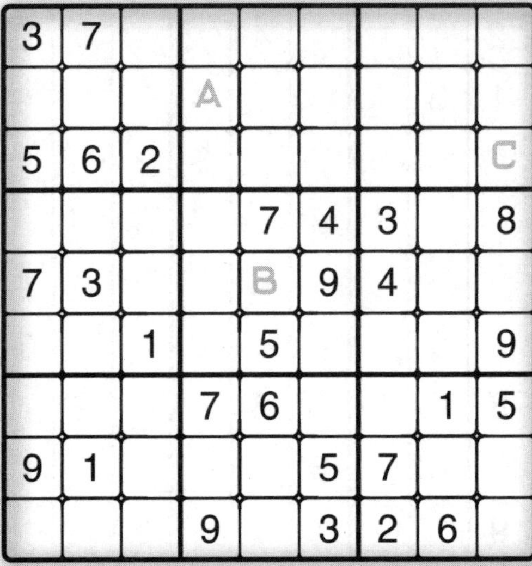

A The insect order Lepidoptera consists of moths, skippers and which insects?

Ants	**5**
Beetles	**1**
Butterflies	**8**

B Which 1984 film, starring Bill Murray and Dan Aykroyd, was advertised with the tagline, 'They're here to save the world!'?

Ghostbusters	**8**
The Goonies	**2**
Three Men and a Baby	**1**

C Julie Andrews starred in which 1964 musical featuring the songs 'Chim Chim Cheree' and 'A Spoonful of Sugar'?

Bedknobs and Broomsticks	**4**
Mary Poppins	**7**
The Sound of Music	**3**

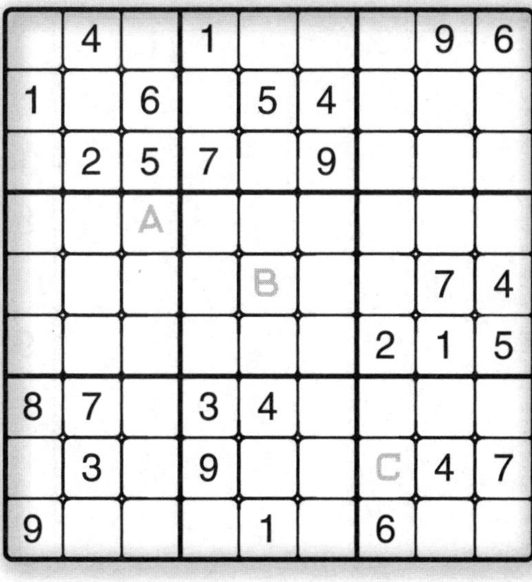

A Greece and Britain have disputed the ownership of the Parthenon Marbles for decades, but by what name are they more commonly known?

The Elton Marbles	**2**
The Elgin Marbles	**7**
The Elvin Marbles	**9**

B The songs 'Getting to Know You' and 'I Whistle a Happy Tune' come from which musical?

South Pacific	**3**
Calamity Jane	**6**
The King and I	**9**

C Which comedian wrote the novels *Popcorn* and *Dead Famous*?

Ben Elton	**1**
Alexei Sayle	**8**
Stephen Fry	**5**

12

shogun

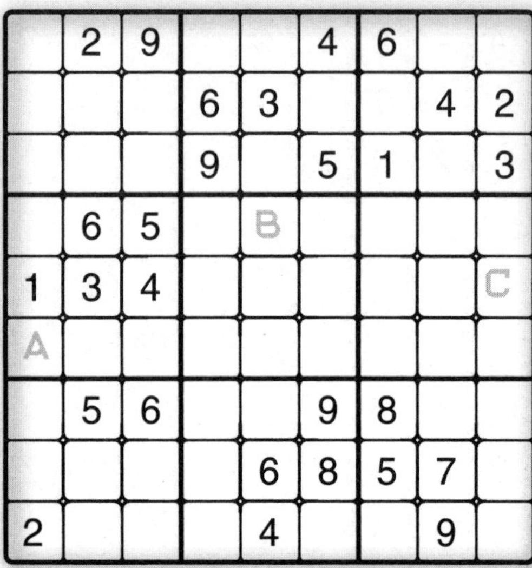

A Whitney Houston's hit cover of 'I Will Always Love You' featured on the soundtrack of which 1992 film?

Ghost	**7**
Beaches	**9**
The Bodyguard	**8**

B What is the capital of Kenya?

Nairobi	**9**
Cape Town	**1**
Lusaka	**2**

C Which American jazz musician was also known by the nickname Satchmo?

Fats Waller	**5**
Thelonious Monk	**6**
Louis Armstrong	**9**

13

shogun

4			B	9		3		
	8	7			2			6
	1	2	8				7	
			2		8		1	7
			3		9		8	4
A				7		9		
	6	3	7				9	
2				1		8		
	9	4			3		C	1

A Babe Ruth is a legendary name in which sport?

Basketball	**8**
Baseball	**5**
American football	**1**

B What nationality was the existentialist novelist and philosopher Albert Camus?

Belgian	**5**
French	**1**
Swiss	**6**

C A googly is associated with which sport?

Cricket	**6**
Golf	**5**
Bowls	**2**

14

shogun

	7			A				6
2		8	4			B		
3					5		9	
			9				6	
	4			2	8			
		1		4				8
	1		8			7		
				3	1		4	5
5		6				C	8	3

A In which US city can the Liberty Bell be found?

Philadelphia	**8**
Boston	**1**
Washington DC	**9**

B In which ocean would you find the Galapagos Islands?

The Atlantic	**1**
The Indian	**5**
The Pacific	**3**

C Which prime minister's father was Alderman Alfred Roberts of Grantham?

Margaret Thatcher	**1**
Harold Macmillan	**2**
Clement Attlee	**9**

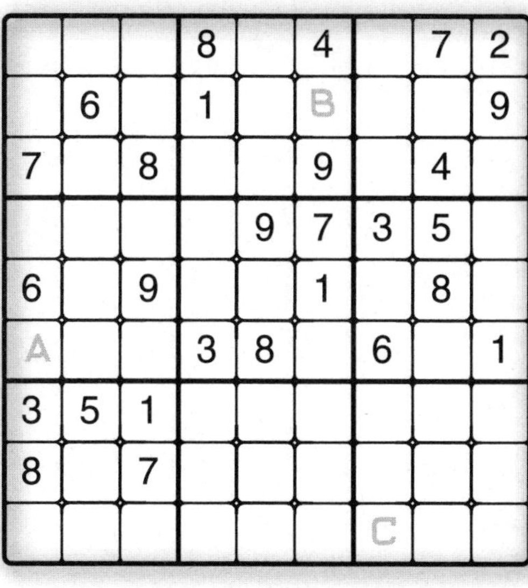

A For what do the letters FHM stand in the name of the men's magazine?

Fun Hits Monthly	**2**
Flash Hot Motors	**5**
For Him Magazine	**4**

B How is William Wainwright, co-producer of Madonna's *Ray of Light* album, better known?

William Orbit	**5**
Fatboy Slim	**2**
Judge Jules	**3**

C In Greek mythology, who captured sailors' minds with their alluring songs, leading them to destruction?

Scylla	**1**
Sirens	**7**
Medusa	**9**

16

shogun

5			8	2				4
	1				6		9	C
		7	4	5		2		
	9	A					5	
4		6			B	9		1
8		5				4		2
9			7	1				5
	4				2		8	
		8	9	6		1		

A Which letters of the alphabet form the normal chromosome pairing of a human male?

XY	**2**
WX	**1**
YZ	**3**

B A Minotaur was a mythical creature that was half-man and half what animal?

Bull	**5**
Goat	**7**
Horse	**8**

C Which playwright wrote the black comedy *Loot*?

John Osborne	**3**
Harold Pinter	**7**
Joe Orton	**8**

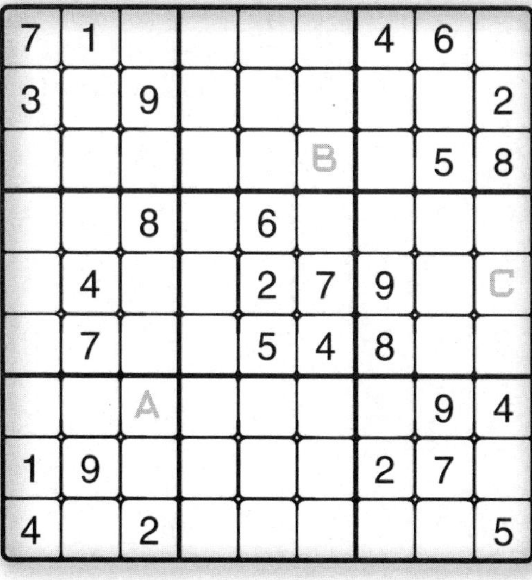

A Harehills and Chapel Allerton are districts of which English city?

Leeds	**7**
Sheffield	**3**
Manchester	**5**

B Which film features Paul Newman and Robert Redford as conmen in 1930s Chicago?

Butch Cassidy and the Sundance Kid	**2**
The Sting	**1**
The Hustler	**6**

C What is the name for the Hindu festival of lights?

Navaratri	**1**
Holi	**3**
Diwali	**6**

18

shogun

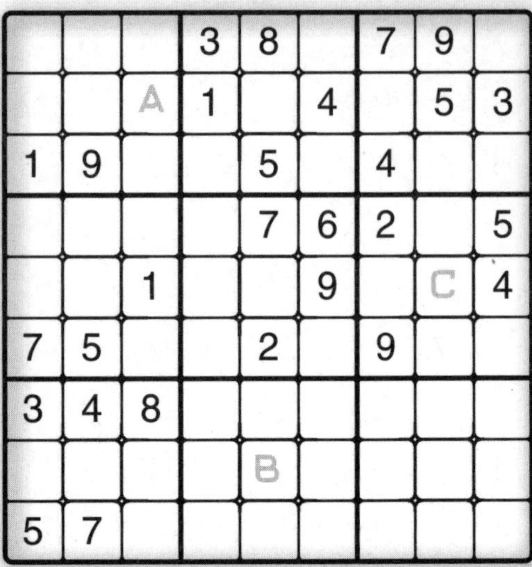

A Which famous American chat-show host starred in the 1985 film *The Color Purple*?

Jerry Springer	**2**
David Letterman	**6**
Oprah Winfrey	**7**

B 'It was the best of times, it was the worst of times' is the opening line of which Charles Dickens novel?

A Tale of Two Cities	**4**
Martin Chuzzlewit	**1**
Bleak House	**9**

C Who played Bottom in the BBC's modern adaptation of *A Midsummer Night's Dream*?

Peter Kay	**3**
Matt Lucas	**8**
Johnny Vegas	**7**

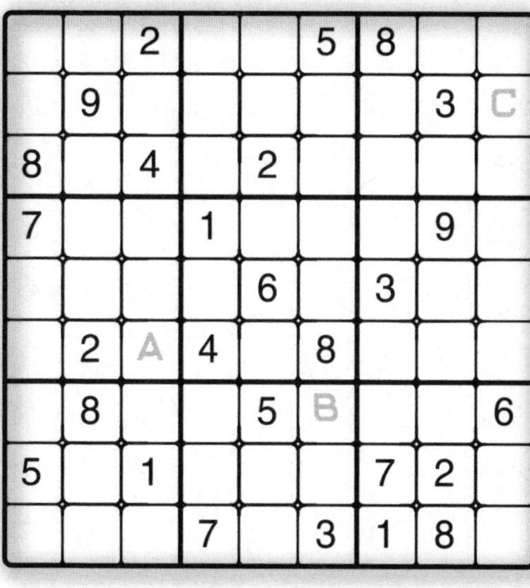

A Morgan Freeman and Tim Robbins starred in which 1995 film, set in a corrupt prison?

The Shawshank Redemption	**3**
O Brother, Where Art Thou?	**5**
The Green Mile	**9**

B Welshman Barry John was an international in which sport?

Rugby league	**2**
Rugby union	**1**
Darts	**4**

C In which American city is the sitcom *Cheers* set?

San Francisco	**1**
Miami	**4**
Boston	**7**

20

shogun

A		3	7		5		9	
		7	3		6		8	
8					1			
9	4					5		
				B		8		6
	7	2					3	1
						3	C	9
5	3					6		
	2	9					5	7

A In which London park were the Queen Elizabeth Gates opened in 1993?

Hyde Park 2

Regents Park 4

St James's Park 6

B What forename was shared by the French kings whose nicknames were 'the Fat', 'the Simple' and 'the Fair'?

Louis 1

Guillaume 3

Charles 7

C Who had a Christmas number one in 1985 with 'Merry Christmas Everyone'?

Slade 2

Cliff Richard 4

Shakin' Stevens 1

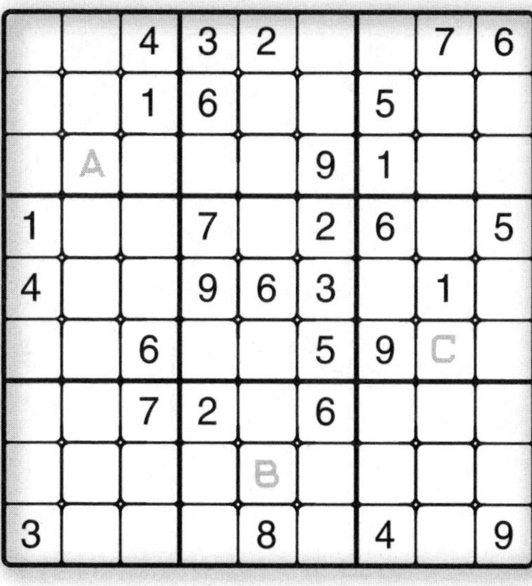

21

shogun

A Which H. G. Wells novel features the Morlocks?

The Invisible Man	**2**
The War of the Worlds	**5**
The Time Machine	**7**

B Which appropriately named horse won the Grand National in the general election year of 1992?

Party Politics	**3**
Polling Booth	**1**
Tory Boy	**7**

C In athletics, which field throwing event is not part of the decathlon?

The javelin	**2**
The hammer	**4**
The discus	**8**

22

shogun

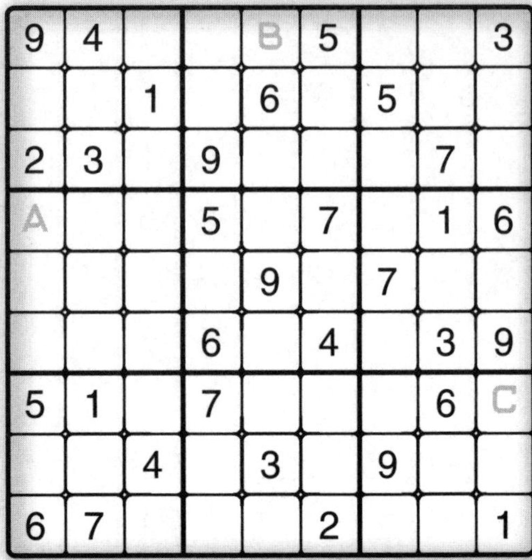

A The US is home to Yuma, usually said to be the world's sunniest place, but which state is it in?

Arizona	**3**
Arkansas	**4**
Idaho	**8**

B Which famous written work begins on 1 January 1660 and ends on 31st May 1669?

Samuel Johnson's Dictionary	**1**
Pepys' Diary	**7**
Domesday Book	**2**

C Which book of the Bible contains the story of Noah and the Great Flood?

Exodus	**2**
Genesis	**8**
Leviticus	**4**

23

shogun

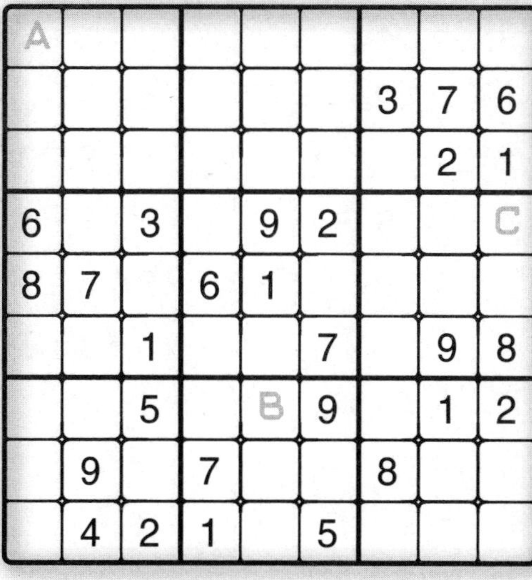

A								
						3	7	6
							2	1
6		3		9	2			C
8	7		6	1				
		1			7		9	8
		5		B	9		1	2
	9		7			8		
	4	2	1		5			

A What is Elton John's real name?

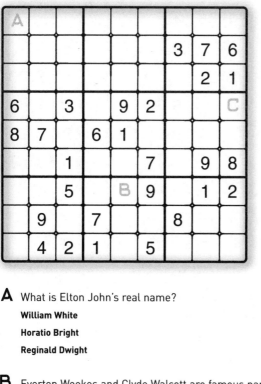

William White	**4**
Horatio Bright	**7**
Reginald Dwight	**2**

B Everton Weekes and Clyde Walcott are famous names in which sport?

Bowls	**3**
Cricket	**6**
Fencing	**8**

C What is the longest river in Africa?

The Nile	**7**
The Zambezi	**4**
The Congo	**5**

24

shogun

7		4						
	1	2				5	3	
6			B				8	9
1		9						C
	6	3				9	5	
4							1	6
	9		3	6		1		
	A			2				7
	7		1	4		3		

A In computing, which single unit does 1024 bytes make?

The megabyte 3

The kilobyte 4

The terabyte 5

B Which Florida city, with around 300 miles of navigable inland waterways, is known as the Venice of America?

Fort Lauderdale 2

Miami 4

Clearwater 7

C What are train drivers called in the US?

Engineers 3

Steamers 2

Wagoneers 8

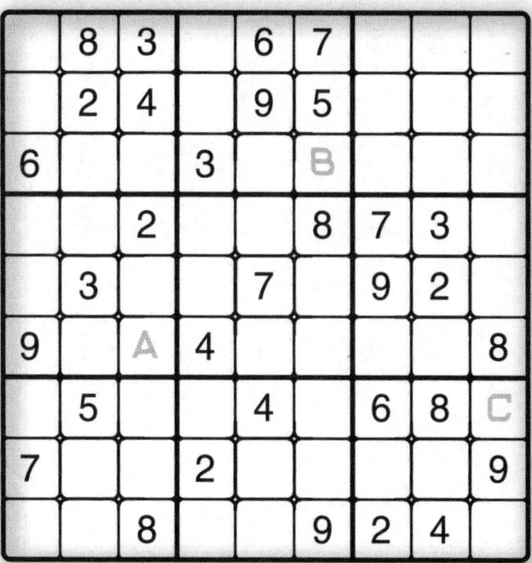

25

shogun

A Resident at Number Ten from 1989 to 1997, spanning the occupation of three prime ministers, what was the name of the Downing Street cat?

Alfred	**1**
Humphrey	**5**
Tiddles	**6**

B Where is the Queen Maud mountain range?

Antarctica	**4**
Australia	**1**
New Zealand	**2**

C Roger Waters rejoined the line-up of which band for the first time in over 20 years at 2005's Live 8 concert in Hyde Park?

King Crimson	**1**
Meat Loaf	**7**
Pink Floyd	**3**

26

shogun

	4	7						8
A								
5			6		9		3	
	7	8	4		2		1	
	2		9					4
4	3	9		1		C	6	
	9		1		B			
7		3		8	4			6
		4	2					1

A In which famous Leonardo da Vinci portrait, exhibited in The Louvre, does the subject have no eyebrows?

The Mona Lisa **3**

The Venus de Milo **2**

The Laughing Cavalier **8**

B Light amplification by stimulated emission of radiation is better known as what?

Strobe light **3**

Radar **5**

Laser **7**

C Which city hosted the 1992 Olympic Games?

Seoul **7**

Atlanta **8**

Barcelona **5**

27

shogun

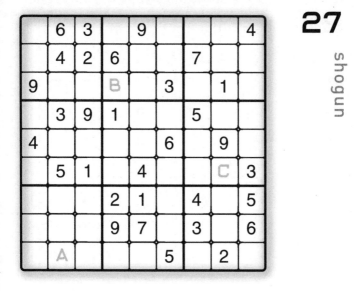

	6	3		9				4
	4	2	6			7		
9			B		3		1	
	3	9	1			5		
4					6		9	
	5	1		4			C	3
			2	1		4		5
			9	7		3		6
	A				5		2	

A Which famously 'unready' monarch found himself on the English throne in AD 1000, the end of the first millennium?

Egbert II **1**

Edmund II **8**

Ethelred II **7**

B Edward J. Smith was the captain of which famous passenger vessel?

QE2 **5**

Lusitania **7**

RMS Titanic **4**

C Michelangelo's fresco *The Creation of Adam* can be found in which building?

St Peter's Basilica **7**

The Pantheon **8**

The Sistine Chapel **6**

28

shogun

1	9		2		3		C	
	4	2	7	6				
6					4	7		9
5		4		8	1			
		6		9			7	
9	A				5	1		4
					B	4		1
						2	3	6

A Romulus and Remus were deposited in a basket as babies. Which animal discovered them and subsequently raised them?

A wolf 2

A bear 3

A wild boar 7

B What was Ebenezer Scrooge's deceased business partner called?

Bob Marley 2

Jacob Marley 7

Uriah Heap 9

C Which country has won the football World Cup a record five times?

Brazil 4

France 5

Germany 8

29

shogun

	3	2	7			9	1	C
9			3			2	7	4
		7		6		3		
A		1				8		
		3		9			4	
8	4			5			3	9
				2		5	8	
					B			
	8	5	1					3

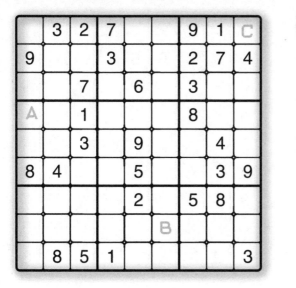

A What natural phenomenon can be described as high, low, neap or spring?

The phases of the moon 5

Sunlight 7

The tides 2

B On a normal UK keyboard, which letter comes between Q and E?

W 3

S 6

A 9

C Colombo is the capital city of which country?

Nepal 8

Peru 5

Sri Lanka 6

30

shogun

		7			4		1	
	3		5	6			C	
	8			2		7		
5		A				1	6	
7			3				2	
		2		1				9
3	5				8	2		
		4			B			
1	2		9					8

A Adam Woodyatt plays which character in *EastEnders*?

Phil Mitchell	**1**
Ian Beale	**3**
Martin Fowler	**8**

B Ian Thorpe and Michael Phelps are famous names in which sport?

Swimming	**1**
Horse racing	**2**
Cycling	**6**

C The cities of Newcastle, Penrith and Liverpool are in which Australian state?

New South Wales	**4**
Victoria	**7**
Queensland	**9**

Round Four

1

emperor

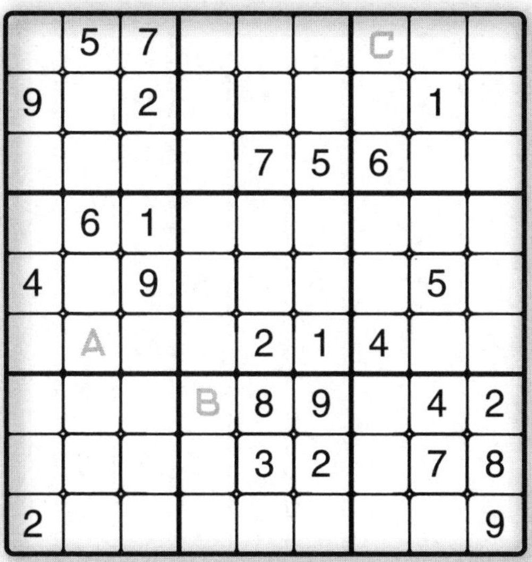

A Rain was the early name of which Manchester Indie Rock band?

Oasis	**7**
The Stone Roses	**3**
Primal Scream	**8**

B Apart from Mercury, which planet in our solar system has no moon?

Venus	**5**
Uranus	**1**
Mars	**6**

C Charles and Lynton are the middle names of which British political figure?

Gordon Brown	**8**
Tony Benn	**9**
Tony Blair	**2**

2

emperor

		1	B					8
2	3			8		9		
				6	2		1	
								9
	9		8		5	7		
4		A				6		
8			9	2			3	
			7		8	1	6	
5				1	3			C

A A cob is a male swan, but what is a female swan called?

A hen 2

A pen 5

A jenny 7

B Which architect designed New York's Guggenheim Museum?

William Van Alen 4

Frank Lloyd Wright 3

Cass Gilbert 5

C Which wild-card entry went on to win the 2001 Wimbledon men's singles title?

Andre Agassi 2

Goran Ivanisevic 7

Pete Sampras 4

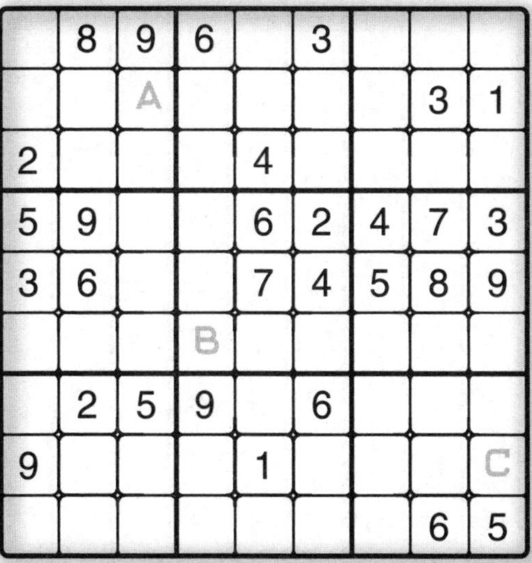

3

emperor

A Which German composer wrote the music for the opera *Tristan and Isolde*, first performed in 1865?

Wagner 4

Schubert 6

Beethoven 7

B African and French are two varieties of which summer bedding plant?

Daisy 1

Geranium 5

Marigold 3

C The teachings of Guru Nanak are the basis for which religion?

Sikhism 8

Hinduism 2

Buddhism 7

4

emperor

	9						4	
		6		4	8			1
	4			7	1	C	3	
5				3	9	6		
4				8	2	3		
A				1	5			
	7			9	4		2	
	5						9	
		9	B	5	3			7

A Richard John Bingham, known as Lucky to his friends, was better known as whom?

Reggie Kray 2

Lord Lucan 9

Dick Turpin 8

B On which West Indian island did calypso music originate?

Trinidad 8

Barbados 1

Jamaica 6

C What is the name for the white of an egg?

The leucogen 5

The albion 9

The albumen 2

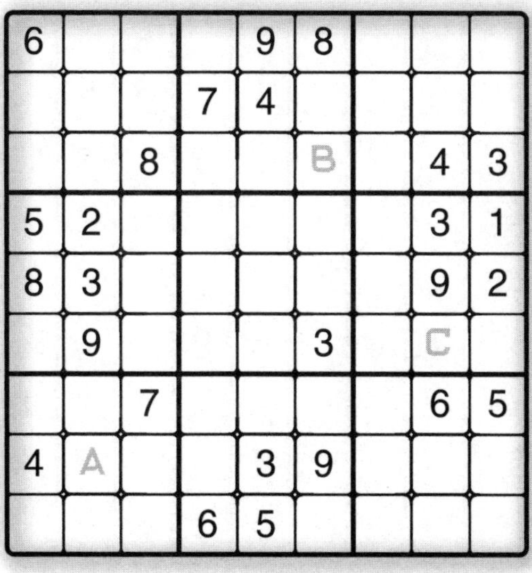

5

emperor

A Which planet, discovered in 1930, that usually orbits outside Neptune, is thought to have a temperature of –200°C?

Pluto	**6**
Saturn	**5**
Uranus	**8**

B What was the name of the Egyptologist who discovered Tutankhamun's tomb in 1922?

Howard Carter	**2**
Zahi Hawass	**1**
Henry Salt	**6**

C What type of pies did Aunt Aggie cook for Desperate Dan in the *Dandy* comic-book stories?

Pork	**5**
Chicken	**7**
Cow	**8**

6

emperor

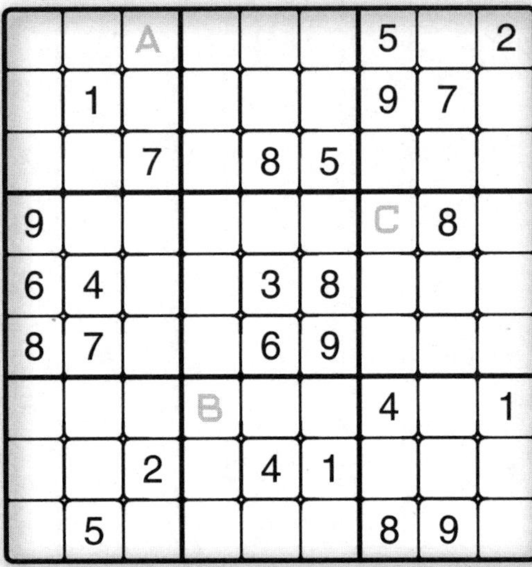

A Who directed the films *Carlito's Way*, *The Untouchables* and *Mission to Mars*?

Francis Ford Coppola **3**

Brian De Palma **9**

Martin Scorsese **8**

B Famed for its knitwear, which is the most southerly of the Shetland Islands?

Islay **2**

Harris **9**

Fair Isle **5**

C In 2005, Tom Cruise starred in the film remake of which H. G. Wells novel?

The War of the Worlds **3**

The Time Machine **1**

The Invisible Man **7**

7

emperor

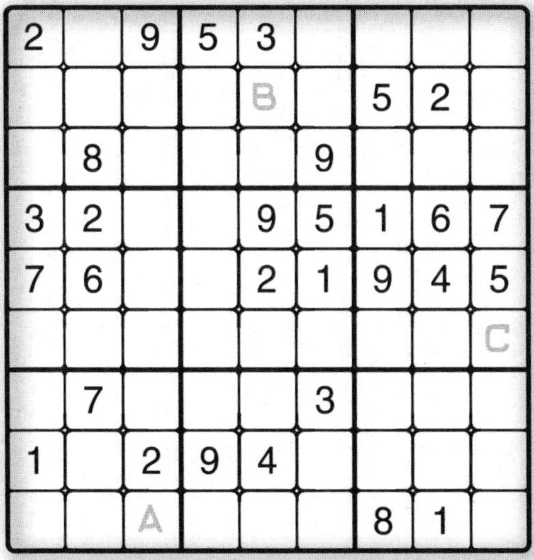

2		9	5	3				
				B		5	2	
	8				9			
3	2			9	5	1	6	7
7	6			2	1	9	4	5
								C
	7				3			
1		2	9	4				
		A				8	1	

A Nick Stone is the hero of novels by which former SAS soldier?

Andy McNab **6**

Shaun Clark **3**

Chris Ryan **4**

B *The Waste Land* is a poem, published in 1922, by which poet?

John Betjeman **1**

Rudyard Kipling **7**

T. S. Eliot **8**

C The west face of which building is featured on the current Bank of England £20 note?

Worcester Cathedral **2**

Westminster Cathedral **3**

York Minster **8**

emperor

	2	6	B		5			
7	1					6		3
9		4			1			2
	A						9	
					8	3		
1	5			9		7		
	4	3					C	6
		1		2	4	9		
			6				1	

A A boxty is an Irish dish made with which vegetable?

Beetroot	**3**
Carrot	**7**
Potato	**6**

B Which Knight of the Realm recently released an album entitled *Chaos and Creation in the Back Yard*?

Sir Cliff Richard	**7**
Sir Paul McCartney	**4**
Sir Elton John	**8**

C In which Swiss city are Grasshoppers Football Club based?

Geneva	**2**
Lucerne	**5**
Zurich	**8**

4								6
	A		4	5				
	1	8			7	4	5	
1	3	9			5	7	6	4
8			1	4		C		9
6			7	3				8
3				B				7
	2	7			4	6	3	
			3	7				

A Epistaxis is the medical term for which disorder?

Gout 7

Nosebleed 9

Earache 6

B In the film *Four Weddings and a Funeral*, who played Hugh Grant's American love interest?

Julia Roberts 1

Andie MacDowell 6

Sandra Bullock 8

C Which nineteenth-century statesman was known as the GOM – Grand Old Man?

Benjamin Disraeli 2

William Gladstone 3

Henry Palmerston 5

10

emperor

3						8		1
A		6	9					
	9			4	1			3
5				2			8	6
				6		9		4
1	6		B			5	3	
		3					C	
	5				7	6	2	
	8			9				

A Which of the Seven Wonders of the Ancient World was the first to be constructed?

The Great Pyramid at Giza 7

The Hanging Gardens of Babylon 2

The Colossus of Rhodes 8

B Who, in February 1962, became the first American astronaut to orbit the Earth?

Alan Shepard 7

Gus Grissom 8

John Glenn 4

C Which English premiership rugby union team play at a home ground nicknamed The Rec?

Bath 5

Sale 1

Northampton 4

Answers

SUDO-Q SUDO-Q

APPRENTICE

1

(A4, B8, C6)

7	1	6	5	9	2	8	3	4
2	4	5	3	6	8	9	1	7
9	3	8	1	4	7	6	5	2
1	7	9	2	3	5	4	6	8
6	8	2	4	1	9	5	7	3
4	5	3	7	8	6	2	9	1
5	6	4	8	7	1	3	2	9
3	2	1	9	5	4	7	8	6
8	9	7	6	2	3	1	4	5

2

(A1, B8, C5)

7	9	2	6	4	3	1	8	5
1	8	6	2	7	5	9	4	3
4	3	5	9	1	8	6	7	2
2	4	7	8	3	9	5	6	1
3	5	8	1	2	6	4	9	7
6	1	9	7	5	4	2	3	8
9	6	1	5	8	7	3	2	4
5	7	3	4	6	2	8	1	9
8	2	4	3	9	1	7	5	6

3

(A5, B7, C6)

1	9	2	8	7	6	5	3	4
7	3	5	1	4	2	8	6	9
4	6	8	5	9	3	7	2	1
2	5	9	4	6	8	1	7	3
6	4	7	3	2	1	9	5	8
8	1	3	7	5	9	6	4	2
5	8	1	2	3	7	4	9	6
3	7	6	9	1	4	2	8	5
9	2	4	6	8	5	3	1	7

4

(A8, B2, C6)

5	6	9	3	1	8	2	4	7
8	2	4	7	6	9	5	3	1
1	3	7	4	5	2	9	6	8
7	8	6	5	9	3	1	2	4
9	4	1	6	2	7	3	8	5
2	5	3	8	4	1	6	7	9
3	9	2	1	8	4	7	5	6
6	7	8	9	3	5	4	1	2
4	1	5	2	7	6	8	9	3

5

(A5, B6, C6)

8	6	9	4	2	7	3	1	5
7	2	1	9	5	3	4	8	6
3	5	4	8	1	6	7	2	9
1	7	2	6	4	8	5	9	3
6	9	5	2	3	1	8	7	4
4	3	8	7	9	5	1	6	2
5	8	6	3	7	2	9	4	1
9	1	7	5	6	4	2	3	8
2	4	3	1	8	9	6	5	7

6

(A6, B4, C1)

9	8	1	4	7	3	2	5	6
2	4	3	1	5	6	7	9	8
7	6	5	2	8	9	3	1	4
4	1	8	5	6	2	9	3	7
5	7	6	3	9	1	4	8	2
3	2	9	7	4	8	5	6	1
1	9	2	6	3	7	8	4	5
6	3	4	8	2	5	1	7	9
8	5	7	9	1	4	6	2	3

7

(A7, B2, C4)

9	3	8	5	4	6	7	1	2
1	6	7	3	9	2	4	5	8
5	4	2	1	7	8	9	3	6
8	2	4	6	5	7	1	9	3
3	7	5	2	1	9	8	6	4
6	1	9	4	8	3	5	2	7
4	9	3	8	6	1	2	7	5
2	8	1	7	3	5	6	4	9
7	5	6	9	2	4	3	8	1

8

(A2, B8, C3)

4	9	3	5	6	7	8	2	1
7	8	2	9	1	3	6	5	4
6	1	5	2	8	4	3	9	7
8	7	4	3	5	1	2	6	9
2	5	9	8	7	6	1	4	3
1	3	6	4	2	9	7	8	5
3	4	7	6	9	2	5	1	8
5	6	1	7	4	8	9	3	2
9	2	8	1	3	5	4	7	6

9

(A6, B8, C7)

9	6	8	3	5	7	2	1	4
1	4	5	2	9	6	3	8	7
3	7	2	4	1	8	6	9	5
8	2	4	5	6	1	7	3	9
7	5	9	8	4	3	1	6	2
6	1	3	9	7	2	5	4	8
5	8	6	7	3	9	4	2	1
4	9	1	6	2	5	8	7	3
2	3	7	1	8	4	9	5	6

10

(A1, B7, C8)

8	4	6	1	2	9	3	5	7
9	1	3	7	6	5	8	2	4
5	7	2	4	3	8	6	1	9
6	5	1	3	8	7	9	4	2
4	3	9	2	5	6	7	8	1
7	2	8	9	1	4	5	3	6
1	8	7	5	9	2	4	6	3
2	6	4	8	7	3	1	9	5
3	9	5	6	4	1	2	7	8

11

(A9, B8, C2)

9	2	3	8	6	1	7	5	4
4	7	8	5	9	2	1	3	6
5	1	6	7	4	3	2	8	9
2	3	1	9	5	8	6	4	7
7	8	5	4	2	6	3	9	1
6	9	4	3	1	7	5	2	8
1	4	2	6	3	9	8	7	5
3	5	7	1	8	4	9	6	2
8	6	9	2	7	5	4	1	3

12

(A6, B7, C3)

3	7	8	4	5	9	1	6	2
5	2	9	1	8	6	3	7	4
6	4	1	7	3	2	8	5	9
2	8	4	9	6	1	7	3	5
1	9	3	5	7	4	6	2	8
7	5	6	8	2	3	9	4	1
8	6	7	2	9	5	4	1	3
9	1	5	3	4	7	2	8	6
4	3	2	6	1	8	5	9	7

13

(A4, B7, C2)

2	8	4	1	6	3	7	5	9
5	6	3	9	8	7	1	4	2
9	7	1	4	5	2	3	8	6
8	3	2	7	1	4	6	9	5
4	9	7	5	3	6	8	2	1
6	1	5	8	2	9	4	3	7
1	4	8	2	7	5	9	6	3
7	5	6	3	9	8	2	1	4
3	2	9	6	4	1	5	7	8

14

(A4, B8, C6)

4	3	5	7	9	6	2	1	8
6	8	1	2	4	5	7	9	3
9	2	7	3	8	1	6	4	5
7	5	4	6	2	3	9	8	1
1	9	3	4	7	8	5	6	2
2	6	8	5	1	9	3	7	4
5	1	9	8	6	2	4	3	7
3	4	6	1	5	7	8	2	9
8	7	2	9	3	4	1	5	6

15

(A1, B5, C8)

2	8	5	3	4	6	7	9	1
4	6	7	9	5	1	3	8	2
1	3	9	7	8	2	4	5	6
8	5	1	4	9	7	2	6	3
9	2	3	6	1	5	8	4	7
6	7	4	2	3	8	9	1	5
7	9	6	5	2	4	1	3	8
5	4	8	1	7	3	6	2	9
3	1	2	8	6	9	5	7	4

16

(A5, B4, C3)

7	3	1	6	4	2	9	5	8
4	6	8	7	9	5	2	3	1
2	9	5	1	3	8	6	7	4
9	5	7	4	6	1	8	2	3
6	8	4	3	2	7	5	1	9
1	2	3	5	8	9	4	6	7
3	4	9	2	1	6	7	8	5
8	7	2	9	5	3	1	4	6
5	1	6	8	7	4	3	9	2

17

(A1, B6, C5)

5	1	4	7	9	6	8	2	3
6	8	9	2	3	4	1	7	5
2	7	3	5	8	1	4	9	6
4	6	7	1	2	8	5	3	9
9	5	8	3	6	7	2	4	1
1	3	2	9	4	5	6	8	7
3	2	1	4	5	9	7	6	8
8	4	5	6	7	3	9	1	2
7	9	6	8	1	2	3	5	4

18

(A4, B6, C8)

7	4	9	8	2	1	6	5	3
5	6	8	9	3	4	1	2	7
3	1	2	7	6	5	4	8	9
9	8	4	5	7	6	2	3	1
2	7	5	3	1	9	8	4	6
1	3	6	4	8	2	7	9	5
4	2	3	6	9	7	5	1	8
8	5	7	1	4	3	9	6	2
6	9	1	2	5	8	3	7	4

19

(A5, B7, C3)

6	9	3	5	8	1	7	2	4
4	2	1	6	7	9	3	5	8
7	8	5	2	3	4	9	6	1
2	3	4	7	9	8	5	1	6
9	1	8	3	5	6	4	7	2
5	6	7	1	4	2	8	3	9
8	7	2	4	6	5	1	9	3
3	4	6	9	1	7	2	8	5
1	5	9	8	2	3	6	4	7

20

(A3, B2, C5)

9	3	6	4	7	1	5	8	2
4	2	5	8	3	6	9	1	7
7	1	8	2	5	9	4	6	3
5	9	7	6	8	3	2	4	1
8	4	3	7	1	2	6	5	9
1	6	2	9	4	5	7	3	8
2	5	9	1	6	8	3	7	4
3	7	1	5	9	4	8	2	6
6	8	4	3	2	7	1	9	5

21

(A7, B3, C2)

9	4	2	1	5	6	3	8	7
5	6	8	2	7	3	9	1	4
7	3	1	8	4	9	5	6	2
2	9	6	5	8	4	7	3	1
8	7	3	6	9	1	2	4	5
4	1	5	3	2	7	6	9	8
6	5	7	9	1	8	4	2	3
1	2	9	4	3	5	8	7	6
3	8	4	7	6	2	1	5	9

22

(A4, B5, C7)

7	3	1	8	4	6	2	5	9
9	8	5	3	2	1	6	7	4
2	4	6	9	5	7	3	8	1
3	6	7	4	1	5	9	2	8
1	9	4	2	6	8	7	3	5
8	5	2	7	3	9	4	1	6
5	7	3	6	8	4	1	9	2
6	1	9	5	7	2	8	4	3
4	2	8	1	9	3	5	6	7

23

(A3, B6, C1)

2	9	8	5	1	4	6	7	3
1	3	5	2	6	7	4	8	9
7	4	6	3	8	9	5	2	1
4	7	2	8	3	1	9	6	5
6	5	1	9	7	2	3	4	8
9	8	3	4	5	6	2	1	7
3	2	9	1	4	8	7	5	6
5	1	7	6	2	3	8	9	4
8	6	4	7	9	5	1	3	2

24

(A1, B4, C8)

8	1	2	6	9	3	7	5	4
9	7	3	5	1	4	2	8	6
6	4	5	8	2	7	9	3	1
1	3	6	9	7	5	8	4	2
7	8	4	2	3	6	1	9	5
2	5	9	4	8	1	6	7	3
3	6	1	7	5	9	4	2	8
4	9	8	3	6	2	5	1	7
5	2	7	1	4	8	3	6	9

25

(A1, B4, C7)

8	3	2	1	7	5	9	4	6
9	1	4	3	6	8	7	5	2
6	5	7	9	2	4	8	1	3
1	2	3	8	4	6	5	9	7
4	7	6	5	9	2	3	8	1
5	9	8	7	3	1	2	6	4
7	6	1	2	8	9	4	3	5
2	8	5	4	1	3	6	7	9
3	4	9	6	5	7	1	2	8

26

(A5, B7, C9)

8	6	3	4	7	5	1	9	2
7	5	1	3	2	9	8	4	6
4	2	9	6	1	8	3	7	5
6	8	5	2	3	7	4	1	9
3	9	4	5	8	1	2	6	7
1	7	2	9	4	6	5	3	8
5	1	7	8	9	4	6	2	3
9	3	8	1	6	2	7	5	4
2	4	6	7	5	3	9	8	1

27

(A3, B5, C6)

9	5	4	8	3	6	1	7	2
6	7	3	4	2	1	8	5	9
8	1	2	9	5	7	6	3	4
7	4	1	2	9	5	3	8	6
2	3	9	6	1	8	7	4	5
5	8	6	3	7	4	9	2	1
3	6	7	5	4	9	2	1	8
4	2	8	1	6	3	5	9	7
1	9	5	7	8	2	4	6	3

28

(A3, B1, C8)

3	4	8	2	1	5	7	9	6
1	6	9	7	3	4	5	2	8
7	5	2	6	9	8	4	1	3
5	8	3	4	6	1	2	7	9
9	7	4	3	8	2	1	6	5
6	2	1	9	5	7	3	8	4
2	9	7	5	4	6	8	3	1
4	1	6	8	2	3	9	5	7
8	3	5	1	7	9	6	4	2

29

(A7, B5, C2)

3	8	9	5	1	4	6	2	7
4	5	7	2	8	6	3	1	9
1	2	6	7	3	9	8	5	4
8	1	2	6	7	5	4	9	3
5	7	4	8	9	3	2	6	1
9	6	3	1	4	2	7	8	5
2	4	8	3	5	1	9	7	6
7	9	5	4	6	8	1	3	2
6	3	1	9	2	7	5	4	8

30

(A4, B3, C2)

6	2	5	8	3	7	4	1	9
9	4	8	6	2	1	3	5	7
3	7	1	4	9	5	6	8	2
5	8	9	7	1	6	2	4	3
7	3	6	2	4	8	5	9	1
2	1	4	9	5	3	7	6	8
4	5	3	1	7	9	8	2	6
1	6	2	3	8	4	9	7	5
8	9	7	5	6	2	1	3	4

1

(A7, B9, C6)

1	6	5	2	8	4	3	7	9
4	8	3	6	7	9	2	1	5
9	2	7	5	3	1	6	4	8
7	4	8	9	1	6	5	3	2
5	3	6	7	4	2	8	9	1
2	1	9	3	5	8	7	6	4
8	7	1	4	6	5	9	2	3
6	5	2	1	9	3	4	8	7
3	9	4	8	2	7	1	5	6

2

(A6, B4, C2)

5	6	8	7	2	1	9	4	3
7	2	3	9	4	6	5	8	1
4	1	9	5	3	8	7	6	2
8	5	6	4	7	3	1	2	9
1	3	2	8	6	9	4	7	5
9	4	7	1	5	2	8	3	6
2	7	1	3	9	4	6	5	8
3	8	4	6	1	5	2	9	7
6	9	5	2	8	7	3	1	4

3

(A6, B4, C5)

1	9	6	5	2	3	8	7	4
8	4	2	7	6	1	9	5	3
3	5	7	4	9	8	6	1	2
7	1	4	3	8	9	5	2	6
6	8	5	1	7	2	4	3	9
2	3	9	6	4	5	1	8	7
5	6	1	2	3	4	7	9	8
9	7	3	8	1	6	2	4	5
4	2	8	9	5	7	3	6	1

4

(A8, B9, C9)

5	2	4	9	7	3	6	1	8
6	1	7	4	8	5	9	2	3
9	3	8	2	1	6	5	7	4
8	7	5	3	4	2	1	6	9
2	9	3	7	6	1	8	4	5
1	4	6	5	9	8	2	3	7
3	6	2	8	5	4	7	9	1
7	5	1	6	3	9	4	8	2
4	8	9	1	2	7	3	5	6

5

(A4, B7, C2)

7	1	8	6	2	9	4	5	3
6	5	3	8	1	4	7	2	9
9	2	4	7	3	5	6	8	1
1	7	5	2	8	3	9	4	6
3	4	2	9	5	6	8	1	7
8	6	9	1	4	7	5	3	2
5	8	7	3	6	2	1	9	4
2	9	1	4	7	8	3	6	5
4	3	6	5	9	1	2	7	8

6

(A1, B5, C9)

2	5	7	9	3	6	4	8	1
4	1	9	8	7	5	2	3	6
3	6	8	2	4	1	9	7	5
8	7	2	3	5	9	1	6	4
1	4	5	6	2	7	8	9	3
6	9	3	1	8	4	5	2	7
5	2	6	7	1	8	3	4	9
7	3	4	5	9	2	6	1	8
9	8	1	4	6	3	7	5	2

7

(A6, B6, C6)

4	9	8	3	7	1	6	2	5
3	6	2	4	8	5	9	7	1
7	5	1	2	9	6	3	4	8
5	8	4	9	2	7	1	3	6
1	3	9	8	6	4	2	5	7
2	7	6	5	1	3	8	9	4
9	2	5	1	4	8	7	6	3
6	1	3	7	5	2	4	8	9
8	4	7	6	3	9	5	1	2

8

(A5, B1, C6)

6	8	5	7	2	3	9	1	4
4	7	9	1	6	8	3	5	2
3	2	1	5	4	9	7	6	8
9	5	2	8	7	1	6	4	3
1	4	7	3	5	6	2	8	9
8	6	3	2	9	4	1	7	5
5	3	6	4	1	2	8	9	7
7	9	8	6	3	5	4	2	1
2	1	4	9	8	7	5	3	6

9

(A5, B9, C2)

6	9	2	4	7	1	5	3	8
3	1	5	2	9	8	6	4	7
8	4	7	6	5	3	9	1	2
4	7	9	8	3	6	2	5	1
5	2	3	1	4	9	8	7	6
1	8	6	5	2	7	4	9	3
7	3	8	9	6	5	1	2	4
2	5	1	3	8	4	7	6	9
9	6	4	7	1	2	3	8	5

10

(A9, B7, C3)

7	8	4	3	2	6	1	5	9
1	3	2	9	7	5	4	6	8
6	5	9	8	1	4	7	2	3
5	7	8	4	6	2	3	9	1
2	6	1	7	9	3	8	4	5
4	9	3	1	5	8	6	7	2
9	1	6	2	8	7	5	3	4
8	4	5	6	3	9	2	1	7
3	2	7	5	4	1	9	8	6

11

(A5, B6, C9)

9	1	8	3	2	7	5	4	6
4	2	7	9	6	5	8	3	1
5	6	3	8	1	4	7	2	9
2	3	1	7	8	6	4	9	5
7	8	9	4	5	1	2	6	3
6	5	4	2	3	9	1	7	8
1	4	6	5	9	2	3	8	7
8	7	5	6	4	3	9	1	2
3	9	2	1	7	8	6	5	4

12

(A9, B3, C7)

5	1	4	9	7	2	6	3	8
9	8	6	4	3	5	1	2	7
3	7	2	1	8	6	9	5	4
4	5	9	6	2	8	7	1	3
8	2	1	7	9	3	5	4	6
7	6	3	5	4	1	2	8	9
1	9	7	8	5	4	3	6	2
6	3	8	2	1	7	4	9	5
2	4	5	3	6	9	8	7	1

13

(A8, B5, C1)

2	6	4	9	8	5	7	3	1
7	9	5	2	1	3	6	4	8
1	8	3	6	7	4	5	9	2
4	2	9	5	6	8	1	7	3
5	3	6	7	2	1	9	8	4
8	1	7	3	4	9	2	6	5
6	7	1	4	3	2	8	5	9
9	4	2	8	5	6	3	1	7
3	5	8	1	9	7	4	2	6

14

(A6, B2, C6)

6	1	8	4	9	7	5	2	3
9	2	7	8	3	5	6	4	1
5	3	4	1	2	6	8	9	7
7	9	2	5	1	8	4	3	6
4	5	3	6	7	9	2	1	8
8	6	1	3	4	2	7	5	9
1	7	5	9	8	4	3	6	2
2	4	9	7	6	3	1	8	5
3	8	6	2	5	1	9	7	4

15

(A4, B8, C9)

4	5	6	2	8	1	3	9	7
9	3	1	6	7	5	8	4	2
8	7	2	3	4	9	6	5	1
5	1	4	7	3	6	2	8	9
7	6	3	8	9	2	5	1	4
2	8	9	1	5	4	7	6	3
3	4	5	9	6	7	1	2	8
1	9	8	5	2	3	4	7	6
6	2	7	4	1	8	9	3	5

16

(A7, B8, C7)

6	8	4	9	2	1	7	3	5
9	2	5	7	6	3	8	1	4
7	1	3	8	4	5	2	6	9
2	5	7	3	1	6	9	4	8
1	6	8	4	5	9	3	7	2
4	3	9	2	7	8	6	5	1
8	9	6	1	3	4	5	2	7
3	7	1	5	8	2	4	9	6
5	4	2	6	9	7	1	8	3

17

(A4, B2, C9)

6	7	4	9	3	1	5	2	8
5	2	1	7	8	6	4	9	3
9	3	8	2	5	4	1	7	6
1	6	7	3	4	5	9	8	2
8	4	9	6	1	2	3	5	7
3	5	2	8	9	7	6	1	4
2	1	3	5	6	8	7	4	9
7	9	5	4	2	3	8	6	1
4	8	6	1	7	9	2	3	5

18

(A8, B7, C3)

3	6	8	1	5	7	4	2	9
9	5	2	8	4	3	1	7	6
4	1	7	9	2	6	8	5	3
7	8	1	2	3	9	5	6	4
2	4	3	6	1	5	7	9	8
5	9	6	4	7	8	2	3	1
6	2	4	5	9	1	3	8	7
8	7	5	3	6	4	9	1	2
1	3	9	7	8	2	6	4	5

19

(A4, B6, C9)

9	1	8	2	6	5	4	7	3
5	3	4	7	8	1	6	9	2
7	6	2	9	4	3	5	1	8
8	5	9	1	7	2	3	4	6
1	2	7	4	3	6	8	5	9
3	4	6	8	5	9	1	2	7
6	9	1	3	2	4	7	8	5
2	7	3	5	1	8	9	6	4
4	8	5	6	9	7	2	3	1

20

(A9, B8, C1)

3	7	1	9	4	2	8	6	5
6	8	2	7	3	5	1	4	9
9	4	5	1	6	8	3	7	2
4	3	7	5	1	6	9	2	8
2	1	9	3	8	4	7	5	6
5	6	8	2	7	9	4	1	3
8	5	4	6	9	7	2	3	1
7	2	3	8	5	1	6	9	4
1	9	6	4	2	3	5	8	7

21

(A8, B1, C6)

6	4	5	7	8	2	9	3	1
3	2	8	1	6	9	7	5	4
1	7	9	5	3	4	6	8	2
7	9	6	4	1	8	3	2	5
4	8	3	2	7	5	1	9	6
2	5	1	6	9	3	4	7	8
5	1	2	3	4	7	8	6	9
9	6	7	8	2	1	5	4	3
8	3	4	9	5	6	2	1	7

22

(A1, B5, C8)

4	2	9	8	7	5	1	3	6
7	6	8	3	4	1	2	5	9
1	5	3	6	9	2	8	4	7
5	3	4	1	8	9	7	6	2
8	1	6	2	3	7	4	9	5
9	7	2	5	6	4	3	8	1
2	8	1	4	5	6	9	7	3
6	4	7	9	2	3	5	1	8
3	9	5	7	1	8	6	2	4

23

(A6, B8, C7)

2	9	8	1	7	4	5	6	3
1	3	5	9	8	6	4	2	7
4	6	7	3	2	5	9	8	1
9	2	1	4	3	8	6	7	5
6	8	3	5	9	7	1	4	2
5	7	4	6	1	2	8	3	9
3	4	9	2	6	1	7	5	8
8	1	6	7	5	3	2	9	4
7	5	2	8	4	9	3	1	6

24

(A2, B9, C3)

8	6	4	3	9	5	7	2	1
1	7	3	8	2	6	4	9	5
9	5	2	7	1	4	8	3	6
3	4	8	5	7	2	1	6	9
6	2	7	9	4	1	3	5	8
5	9	1	6	3	8	2	4	7
4	3	6	1	8	9	5	7	2
2	8	9	4	5	7	6	1	3
7	1	5	2	6	3	9	8	4

25
(A4, B3, C5)

2	4	6	5	8	3	9	7	1
5	1	7	4	2	9	3	8	6
3	9	8	1	6	7	4	2	5
7	5	9	8	3	6	2	1	4
6	3	1	9	4	2	7	5	8
4	8	2	7	5	1	6	3	9
1	7	3	6	9	5	8	4	2
9	2	4	3	1	8	5	6	7
8	6	5	2	7	4	1	9	3

26
(A9, B1, C8)

4	9	6	3	5	1	8	2	7
5	8	1	7	2	4	3	9	6
7	3	2	8	6	9	4	5	1
9	7	8	2	4	3	1	6	5
6	5	4	9	1	8	7	3	2
1	2	3	6	7	5	9	8	4
2	6	9	4	3	7	5	1	8
3	1	7	5	8	6	2	4	9
8	4	5	1	9	2	6	7	3

27
(A9, B8, C7)

1	7	3	6	9	5	2	4	8
9	8	2	4	7	1	5	6	3
5	6	4	8	3	2	1	9	7
7	3	9	5	2	4	6	8	1
4	2	1	9	8	6	7	3	5
6	5	8	3	1	7	4	2	9
8	4	6	1	5	3	9	7	2
2	9	5	7	6	8	3	1	4
3	1	7	2	4	9	8	5	6

28
(A7, B1, C2)

5	4	2	7	3	9	8	1	6
8	9	1	2	5	6	3	7	4
3	7	6	4	8	1	9	2	5
9	6	5	1	2	8	4	3	7
2	1	7	6	4	3	5	9	8
4	8	3	5	9	7	2	6	1
7	3	4	9	6	5	1	8	2
1	2	9	8	7	4	6	5	3
6	5	8	3	1	2	7	4	9

29
(A5, B2, C1)

1	2	6	9	8	5	4	3	7
3	8	5	7	4	6	9	2	1
4	9	7	2	3	1	8	5	6
8	6	9	3	7	4	5	1	2
7	3	2	1	5	8	6	9	4
5	1	4	6	9	2	7	8	3
6	7	8	5	1	3	2	4	9
2	5	3	4	6	9	1	7	8
9	4	1	8	2	7	3	6	5

30
(A8, B3, C6)

1	2	3	9	6	8	7	4	5
5	7	9	4	3	2	8	6	1
6	8	4	1	5	7	2	3	9
9	4	7	5	8	6	1	2	3
2	1	8	3	7	4	9	5	6
3	6	5	2	9	1	4	7	8
7	5	2	8	1	3	6	9	4
8	9	6	7	4	5	3	1	2
4	3	1	6	2	9	5	8	7

1
(A6, B2, C5)

1	5	3	6	2	4	9	7	8
7	8	2	5	1	9	6	4	3
9	4	6	3	7	8	1	2	5
6	3	1	4	9	2	5	8	7
4	9	7	1	8	5	2	3	6
5	2	8	7	3	6	4	1	9
3	1	5	2	6	7	8	9	4
2	6	9	8	4	3	7	5	1
8	7	4	9	5	1	3	6	2

2
(A3, B5, C4)

8	3	4	7	1	5	2	6	9
9	2	6	3	4	8	5	7	1
5	7	1	9	2	6	3	8	4
1	9	7	4	8	2	6	3	5
6	4	2	1	5	3	8	9	7
3	5	8	6	9	7	1	4	2
4	6	3	2	7	1	9	5	8
7	1	5	8	6	9	4	2	3
2	8	9	5	3	4	7	1	6

3
(A1, B5, C7)

7	1	2	5	9	8	6	3	4
4	9	6	1	3	7	5	8	2
5	3	8	4	2	6	7	9	1
9	7	5	3	6	4	2	1	8
1	6	3	2	8	5	4	7	9
2	8	4	9	7	1	3	5	6
6	2	7	8	1	3	9	4	5
3	5	1	6	4	9	8	2	7
8	4	9	7	5	2	1	6	3

4
(A8, B1, C3)

8	5	7	2	1	9	6	4	3
3	4	9	6	5	8	1	7	2
6	1	2	3	4	7	8	5	9
9	2	6	4	3	5	7	8	1
1	7	5	9	8	6	3	2	4
4	8	3	1	7	2	5	9	6
2	3	8	7	9	1	4	6	5
7	9	4	5	6	3	2	1	8
5	6	1	8	2	4	9	3	7

5
(A7, B1, C8)

2	9	8	3	4	1	6	5	7
3	4	5	6	7	8	1	9	2
6	7	1	5	9	2	8	4	3
7	2	6	9	3	5	4	8	1
1	8	9	4	2	6	3	7	5
5	3	4	8	1	7	2	6	9
8	1	2	7	5	4	9	3	6
9	6	7	1	8	3	5	2	4
4	5	3	2	6	9	7	1	8

6
(A5, B4, C2)

7	8	4	2	9	1	3	6	5
6	3	2	8	7	5	4	9	1
1	5	9	3	6	4	2	7	8
3	9	8	4	2	7	1	5	6
2	4	6	1	5	8	9	3	7
5	7	1	9	3	6	8	4	2
4	6	3	5	1	2	7	8	9
9	2	5	7	8	3	6	1	4
8	1	7	6	4	9	5	2	3

7
(A2, B6, C7)

8	6	5	7	9	4	2	1	3
7	9	2	6	1	3	5	8	4
1	4	3	2	8	5	7	9	6
4	1	6	5	2	7	8	3	9
3	5	9	8	4	6	1	2	7
2	7	8	1	3	9	4	6	5
5	8	7	9	6	1	3	4	2
9	2	4	3	5	8	6	7	1
6	3	1	4	7	2	9	5	8

8
(A6, B8, C7)

9	8	2	5	6	3	7	4	1
6	3	7	1	9	4	8	2	5
1	4	5	8	2	7	3	6	9
5	1	6	4	3	8	9	7	2
4	7	8	2	5	9	6	1	3
2	9	3	7	1	6	4	5	8
8	6	1	3	4	2	5	9	7
7	5	4	9	8	1	2	3	6
3	2	9	6	7	5	1	8	4

9
(A2, B1, C9)

2	5	8	6	4	7	3	1	9
9	3	7	2	1	5	8	4	6
1	6	4	9	3	8	2	7	5
6	7	1	8	9	3	4	5	2
8	4	2	5	6	1	7	9	3
5	9	3	4	7	2	6	8	1
3	1	6	7	5	4	9	2	8
7	8	5	3	2	9	1	6	4
4	2	9	1	8	6	5	3	7

10
(A8, B8, C7)

3	7	8	5	9	6	1	4	2
1	9	4	8	2	7	5	3	6
5	6	2	4	3	1	8	9	7
6	2	9	1	7	4	3	5	8
7	3	5	6	8	9	4	2	1
4	8	1	3	5	2	6	7	9
2	4	3	7	6	8	9	1	5
9	1	6	2	4	5	7	8	3
8	5	7	9	1	3	2	6	4

11
(A7, B9, C1)

7	4	8	1	3	2	5	9	6
1	9	6	8	5	4	7	2	3
3	2	5	7	6	9	4	8	1
5	1	7	4	2	8	3	6	9
2	6	3	5	9	1	8	7	4
4	8	9	6	7	3	2	1	5
8	7	1	3	4	6	9	5	2
6	3	2	9	8	5	1	4	7
9	5	4	2	1	7	6	3	8

12
(A8, B9, C9)

3	2	9	1	8	4	6	5	7
5	8	1	6	3	7	9	4	2
6	4	7	9	2	5	1	8	3
7	6	5	4	9	3	2	1	8
1	3	4	8	5	2	7	6	9
8	9	2	7	1	6	4	3	5
4	5	6	3	7	9	8	2	1
9	1	3	2	6	8	5	7	4
2	7	8	5	4	1	3	9	6

13

(A5, B1, C6)

4	5	6	1	9	7	3	2	8
9	8	7	4	3	2	1	5	6
3	1	2	8	6	5	4	7	9
6	3	9	2	4	8	5	1	7
7	2	1	3	5	9	6	8	4
5	4	8	6	7	1	9	3	2
1	6	3	7	8	4	2	9	5
2	7	5	9	1	6	8	4	3
8	9	4	5	2	3	7	6	1

14

(A8, B3, C1)

1	7	9	3	8	2	4	5	6
2	5	8	4	6	9	3	1	7
3	6	4	1	7	5	8	9	2
8	3	2	9	1	7	5	6	4
7	4	5	6	2	8	9	3	1
6	9	1	5	4	3	2	7	8
4	1	3	8	5	6	7	2	9
9	8	7	2	3	1	6	4	5
5	2	6	7	9	4	1	8	3

15

(A4, B5, C7)

5	9	3	8	6	4	1	7	2
2	6	4	1	7	5	8	3	9
7	1	8	2	3	9	5	4	6
1	8	2	6	9	7	3	5	4
6	3	9	4	5	1	2	8	7
4	7	5	3	8	2	6	9	1
3	5	1	7	4	6	9	2	8
8	2	7	9	1	3	4	6	5
9	4	6	5	2	8	7	1	3

16

(A2, B5, C8)

5	6	9	8	2	1	3	7	4
2	1	4	3	7	6	5	9	8
3	8	7	4	5	9	2	1	6
1	9	2	6	4	3	8	5	7
4	7	6	2	8	5	9	3	1
8	3	5	1	9	7	4	6	2
9	2	3	7	1	8	6	4	5
6	4	1	5	3	2	7	8	9
7	5	8	9	6	4	1	2	3

17

(A7, B1, C6)

7	1	5	2	3	8	4	6	9
3	8	9	5	4	6	7	1	2
2	6	4	7	9	1	3	5	8
9	2	8	1	6	3	5	4	7
5	4	1	8	2	7	9	3	6
6	7	3	9	5	4	8	2	1
8	5	7	3	1	2	6	9	4
1	9	6	4	8	5	2	7	3
4	3	2	6	7	9	1	8	5

18

(A7, B4, C7)

4	6	5	3	8	2	7	9	1
2	8	7	1	9	4	6	5	3
1	9	3	6	5	7	4	8	2
8	3	9	4	7	6	2	1	5
6	2	1	5	3	9	8	7	4
7	5	4	8	2	1	9	3	6
3	4	8	9	6	5	1	2	7
9	1	2	7	4	3	5	6	8
5	7	6	2	1	8	3	4	9

19

(A3, B1, C7)

1	7	2	3	9	5	8	6	4
6	9	5	8	1	4	2	3	7
8	3	4	6	2	7	5	1	9
7	5	6	1	3	2	4	9	8
4	1	8	5	6	9	3	7	2
9	2	3	4	7	8	6	5	1
3	8	7	2	5	1	9	4	6
5	4	1	9	8	6	7	2	3
2	6	9	7	4	3	1	8	5

20

(A2, B7, C1)

2	6	3	7	8	5	1	9	4
4	1	7	3	9	6	2	8	5
8	9	5	4	2	1	7	6	3
9	4	8	1	6	3	5	7	2
3	5	1	2	7	9	8	4	6
6	7	2	8	5	4	9	3	1
7	8	6	5	4	2	3	1	9
5	3	4	9	1	7	6	2	8
1	2	9	6	3	8	4	5	7

21

(A7, B3, C4)

9	5	4	3	2	1	8	7	6
2	3	1	6	7	8	5	9	4
6	7	8	4	5	9	1	3	2
1	9	3	7	4	2	6	8	5
4	8	5	9	6	3	2	1	7
7	2	6	8	1	5	9	4	3
8	4	7	2	9	6	3	5	1
5	6	9	1	3	4	7	2	8
3	1	2	5	8	7	4	6	9

22

(A3, B7, C8)

9	4	6	2	7	5	1	8	3
7	8	1	4	6	3	5	9	2
2	3	5	9	1	8	6	7	4
3	9	2	5	8	7	4	1	6
4	6	8	3	9	1	7	2	5
1	5	7	6	2	4	8	3	9
5	1	3	7	4	9	2	6	8
8	2	4	1	3	6	9	5	7
6	7	9	8	5	2	3	4	1

23

(A2, B6, C7)

2	6	7	3	4	1	5	8	9
9	1	4	2	5	8	3	7	6
5	3	8	9	7	6	4	2	1
6	5	3	8	9	2	1	4	7
8	7	9	6	1	4	2	3	5
4	2	1	5	3	7	6	9	8
3	8	5	4	6	9	7	1	2
1	9	6	7	2	3	8	5	4
7	4	2	1	8	5	9	6	3

24

(A4, B2, C3)

7	8	4	5	9	3	2	6	1
9	1	2	7	8	6	5	3	4
6	3	5	2	1	4	7	8	9
1	2	9	6	5	8	4	7	3
8	6	3	4	7	1	9	5	2
4	5	7	9	3	2	8	1	6
2	9	8	3	6	7	1	4	5
3	4	1	8	2	5	6	9	7
5	7	6	1	4	9	3	2	8

25

(A5, B4, C3)

5	8	3	1	6	7	4	9	2
1	2	4	8	9	5	3	7	6
6	9	7	3	2	4	8	5	1
4	6	2	9	1	8	7	3	5
8	3	1	5	7	6	9	2	4
9	7	5	4	3	2	1	6	8
2	5	9	7	4	1	6	8	3
7	4	6	2	8	3	5	1	9
3	1	8	6	5	9	2	4	7

26

(A3, B7, C5)

9	4	7	3	2	1	6	5	8
3	6	1	8	7	5	4	2	9
5	8	2	6	4	9	1	3	7
6	7	8	4	5	2	9	1	3
1	2	5	9	6	3	7	8	4
4	3	9	7	1	8	5	6	2
2	9	6	1	3	7	8	4	5
7	1	3	5	8	4	2	9	6
8	5	4	2	9	6	3	7	1

27

(A7, B4, C6)

1	6	3	7	9	2	8	5	4
5	4	2	6	8	1	7	3	9
9	8	7	4	5	3	6	1	2
6	3	9	1	2	7	5	4	8
4	2	8	5	3	6	1	9	7
7	5	1	8	4	9	2	6	3
3	9	6	2	1	8	4	7	5
2	1	5	9	7	4	3	8	6
8	7	4	3	6	5	9	2	1

28

(A2, B7, C4)

1	9	7	2	5	3	6	4	8
8	4	2	7	6	9	5	1	3
6	3	5	8	1	4	7	2	9
5	7	4	6	8	1	3	9	2
3	1	6	4	9	2	8	7	5
9	2	8	3	7	5	1	6	4
2	6	9	5	3	7	4	8	1
7	5	1	9	4	8	2	3	6
4	8	3	1	2	6	9	5	7

29

(A2, B3, C6)

5	3	2	7	4	8	9	1	6
9	6	8	3	1	5	2	7	4
4	1	7	9	6	2	3	5	8
2	9	1	4	3	7	8	6	5
7	5	3	8	9	6	1	4	2
8	4	6	2	5	1	7	3	9
3	7	9	6	2	4	5	8	1
1	2	4	5	8	3	6	9	7
6	8	5	1	7	9	4	2	3

30

(A3, B1, C4)

2	6	7	8	3	4	9	1	5
9	3	1	5	6	7	8	4	2
4	8	5	1	2	9	7	3	6
5	9	3	4	8	2	1	6	7
7	1	8	3	9	6	5	2	4
6	4	2	7	1	5	3	8	9
3	5	9	6	4	8	2	7	1
8	7	4	2	5	1	6	9	3
1	2	6	9	7	3	4	5	8

1

(A7, B5, C2)

6	5	7	1	9	3	2	8	4
9	3	2	8	4	6	7	1	5
1	4	8	2	7	5	6	9	3
3	6	1	4	5	8	9	2	7
4	2	9	3	6	7	8	5	1
8	7	5	9	2	1	4	3	6
7	1	6	5	8	9	3	4	2
5	9	4	6	3	2	1	7	8
2	8	3	7	1	4	5	6	9

2

(A5, B3, C7)

6	5	1	3	9	4	2	7	8
2	3	4	1	8	7	9	5	6
7	8	9	5	6	2	3	1	4
3	2	8	6	7	1	5	4	9
1	9	6	8	4	5	7	2	3
4	7	5	2	3	9	6	8	1
8	1	7	9	2	6	4	3	5
9	4	3	7	5	8	1	6	2
5	6	2	4	1	3	8	9	7

3

(A4, B3, C8)

1	8	9	6	2	3	7	5	4
6	5	4	7	9	8	2	3	1
2	3	7	5	4	1	8	9	6
5	9	1	8	6	2	4	7	3
3	6	2	1	7	4	5	8	9
7	4	8	3	5	9	6	1	2
8	2	5	9	3	6	1	4	7
9	7	6	4	1	5	3	2	8
4	1	3	2	8	7	9	6	5

4

(A9, B8, C2)

7	9	1	3	2	6	8	4	5
2	3	6	5	4	8	9	7	1
8	4	5	9	7	1	2	3	6
5	8	2	7	3	9	6	1	4
4	1	7	6	8	2	3	5	9
9	6	3	4	1	5	7	8	2
6	7	8	1	9	4	5	2	3
3	5	4	2	6	7	1	9	8
1	2	9	8	5	3	4	6	7

5

(A6, B2, C8)

6	4	2	3	9	8	1	5	7
3	5	9	7	4	1	8	2	6
1	7	8	5	6	2	9	4	3
5	2	4	9	8	6	7	3	1
8	3	1	4	7	5	6	9	2
7	9	6	2	1	3	5	8	4
9	1	7	8	2	4	3	6	5
4	6	5	1	3	9	2	7	8
2	8	3	6	5	7	4	1	9

6

(A9, B5, C3)

4	8	9	7	1	6	5	3	2
5	1	6	3	2	4	9	7	8
2	3	7	9	8	5	1	6	4
9	2	1	4	5	7	3	8	6
6	4	5	2	3	8	7	1	9
8	7	3	1	6	9	2	4	5
7	6	8	5	9	3	4	2	1
3	9	2	8	4	1	6	5	7
1	5	4	6	7	2	8	9	3

7

(A6, B8, C2)

2	1	9	5	3	4	6	7	8
6	4	3	1	8	7	5	2	9
5	8	7	2	6	9	4	3	1
3	2	4	8	9	5	1	6	7
7	6	8	3	2	1	9	4	5
9	5	1	4	7	6	3	8	2
8	7	5	6	1	3	2	9	4
1	3	2	9	4	8	7	5	6
4	9	6	7	5	2	8	1	3

8

(A6, B4, C8)

8	2	6	4	3	5	1	7	9
7	1	5	2	8	9	6	4	3
9	3	4	7	6	1	8	5	2
3	6	7	1	4	2	5	9	8
4	9	2	5	7	8	3	6	1
1	5	8	3	9	6	7	2	4
5	4	3	9	1	7	2	8	6
6	7	1	8	2	4	9	3	5
2	8	9	6	5	3	4	1	7

9

(A9, B6, C3)

4	5	3	2	1	8	9	7	6
7	9	6	4	5	3	1	8	2
2	1	8	6	9	7	4	5	3
1	3	9	8	2	5	7	6	4
8	7	5	1	4	6	3	2	9
6	4	2	7	3	9	5	1	8
3	8	4	5	6	1	2	9	7
5	2	7	9	8	4	6	3	1
9	6	1	3	7	2	8	4	5

10

(A7, B4, C5)

3	2	4	7	5	6	8	9	1
7	1	6	9	8	3	2	4	5
8	9	5	2	4	1	7	6	3
5	4	7	3	2	9	1	8	6
2	3	8	1	6	5	9	7	4
1	6	9	4	7	8	5	3	2
9	7	3	6	1	2	4	5	8
4	5	1	8	3	7	6	2	9
6	8	2	5	9	4	3	1	7

Sudo-Q puzzles supplied by www.PUZZLE.tv